This book offer
students talk, y
listened, and th
and a model for how to foster it.

—Mike Rose, PhD
Research Professor
UCLA Graduate School of Education and Information Studies
Author, *Back to School: Why Everyone Deserves
a Second Chance at Education*

Casazza and Silverman go right to the source, the purest source, the student voice, to find out what truly works for students. This is what we as educators need to hear and heed if we truly want to succeed in our efforts to improve education.

—Robin Ozz, MEd
President, National Association for Developmental
Education (2015–2017)
Faculty Director of Developmental Education and
English Faculty at Phoenix College

Casazza and Silverman have captured, in the voices of students, the key to academic success. And it has little to do with prior achievement or ability. The theme that reverberates throughout this mesmerizing volume is that knowing that someone believes that you *can* succeed, and having a support system available, can provide the motivation for overcoming any obstacles. This is a must-read for anyone interested in closing the gap between the academic success rates of traditional and nontraditional students, at any level.

—Saundra McGuire, PhD
Former Assistant Vice Chancellor and Professor of Chemistry,
Louisiana State University
Director Emerita, LSU Center for Academic Success
Author, *Teach Students How to Learn*

In *Student Voices: We Believe in You,* Martha Casazza and Sharon Silverman honor the notion that each student is an individual with unique needs. The authentic narratives of student voices and the Believe in You model presented in this must-read book will inspire every educator to help students develop abilities of the heart and mind so that each can reach their own potential.

—Dr. Russ Hodges, Associate Professor, Texas State University
Chair, Council of Learning Assistance and Developmental
Education Associations (2007–2014)

Casazza and Silverman have done it again; in groundbreaking work using students' voices, they spotlight the factors that help students persist through significant barriers to academic success. In their model Believe in You, they describe the universal and essential interplay between a student's belief in herself and her abilities to grow, learn, and develop and the necessity of support from family and college—whether that is an instructor, a mentor, or persons in a program or center. It is, however, the stories directly from students that make this a fascinating must-read. Enjoy—and use what you learn in your own work with students, children, or clients.

—Jane A. Neuburger, CLADEA Fellow (2006)
NADE Accreditation Commission
Former Director of the Tutoring & Study Center, Syracuse University
Former President, National Association for Developmental Education
Former President, New York College Learning Skills Association

Student
Voices

We Believe in You

Martha E. Casazza and Sharon L. Silverman

STUDENT VOICES
WE BELIEVE IN YOU

iUniverse books may be ordered through booksellers or by contacting:

iUniverse
1663 Liberty Drive
Bloomington, IN 47403
www.iuniverse.com
1-800-Authors (1-800-288-4677)

ISBN: 978-1-5320-2974-5 (sc)
ISBN: 978-1-5320-2973-8 (e)

Library of Congress Control Number: 2017914722

Print information available on the last page.

iUniverse rev. date: 12/12/2017

CONTENTS

FOREWORD

If you want to know how students succeed when success seems elusive, read this book. As chancellor of the City Colleges of Chicago, I personally know how the odds are often stacked against student success. Today's students are too often burdened with financial stress, family obligations, and emotional distress. Casazza and Silverman listened to their stories and learned how they overcame countless challenges to reach their goals. Not only did they listen and learn, but they combined their extensive expertise to ground the stories in theory and create principles and strategies to use with all students.

The authors dedicated decades of practice to ensuring that traditionally underserved populations have access to education and support systems to ensure their success. They both understand the significance of putting students at the center of their work and listening to student stories to inform their practice.

Dr. Casazza opened opportunities for the Latino community when she served as dean at National-Louis University. She worked with community leaders to understand local needs and set a strategic vision for her college through Proyecto Comunidad. She continued these partnerships when she became the vice president of academic affairs at the Adler School of Psychology, where the mission revolved around taking responsibility for social justice. At the same time, Dr. Silverman was working with the Chicago City Colleges at Truman College to design an academic support system for all students. She also directed an award-winning learning center at Loyola University Chicago. Together, they worked with Instituto del Progreso Latino to help create a two-year college based on the needs of the community.

Casazza and Silverman know the value of listening to our students and learning from them. In this book, *Student Voices: We Believe in You*, they tell the stories of students who faced significant obstacles yet met their goals through persistence, emotional awareness, and self-efficacy. They remind us that having someone who believes in you makes all the difference. The authors offer five principles for educational practice based on the stories and also provide examples of specific instructional strategies.

You will find the student stories in this book inspiring and filled with hope. When you finish reading it, you will want to hear more. You will also be reminded how important it is to understand our students from a holistic perspective.

Juan Salgado, MUP
Chancellor, Chicago City Colleges
Recipient, MacArthur Genius award (2015)

PREFACE

We've dedicated our careers to supporting and encouraging student success. We know the learning theories. We study the research. We share our expertise here and abroad. We write about developing learning centers and academic support programs. The National Association for Developmental Education (NADE) has even included two of our publications among its top ten recommended books. NADE suggests one of these books for those applying for certification of a learning support program.

Still, we wonder: How closely does our knowledge match the reality of students who reach their goals against great odds? We decided to ask the students themselves.

We marvel at students who succeed in the face of significant barriers. Why don't they just give up? What feeds their perseverance? Our professional colleagues gave us the names of students who succeeded while overcoming major challenges. We reached out to those students. We interviewed them, and they rewarded us with the moving stories you will read in this book. You can hear some of these stories and more at www.trppassociates.com.

These students inspired us. They motivated us to emphasize the importance of knowing the whole student and not just a grade point average or number of terms on probation. With each interview, we became more and more convinced of the connection between their experiences and the knowledge we possess. We can attribute their success to what we already know but too often do not recognize or translate this into sustainable educational practice.

Throughout the interviews, students told us having someone believe in them was the defining element in their success. We call this the Believe in You factor and connect it to what we know about persistence, emotional awareness, and self-efficacy. At the end of each chapter, we provide reflective questions to promote further inquiry and encourage the use of principles and strategies based on what we've learned from these amazing students. As you read these questions, we invite you to consider what really makes a difference in the lives of your students and believe in them.

ACKNOWLEDGMENTS

This book would not be possible without the wonderful students who enthusiastically agreed to tell their stories. The students here are a small but representative sample of the total population we interviewed, but they all truly wanted to give back by telling others how they achieved their goals. They were recommended to us by a cohort of our professional colleagues around the world, including Saundra McGuire, Paul Simpson, John Zubizarreta, Sheilagh Grills, and Teri Maddox.

We are truly indebted to Tina Mote, who spent hours transcribing every interview and who also helped analyze the initial data that led to the Believe in You model. Without Brian Block's expertise, we would not have been able to make the audiotapes available on our website. He compiled our edits and formatted them.

Chapter 1

The Power of Stories

My mom believed in me, and the faculty
believed in me, and I can do this.

W E ARE SURROUNDED by voices. Every day, there are
multiple voices competing for our attention. They
come at us through electronic devices like smartphones,
televisions, and laptops. We encounter them as we walk
down the street or take public transportation. We try to sort
through them quickly, deleting some and integrating others
to try to make sense of them, but are we really listening?
How often do we actually stop and listen to those voices that
have stories to tell? How often do we try to find meaning by
asking others to tell us their stories?

Listening to stories is what this book is all about. For the
last five years, we have been asking students to tell us their
stories. We wanted to pay attention to their voices and share
what we heard with others. Their stories are inspiring. They
tell us more about the reasons for student success than do
the piles of quantitative data we have collected throughout
the years.

Who Are the Students?

We talked to students who had faced challenges when they first started thinking about college but persisted and achieved their goals. The barriers included being a first-generation student, coming from a school system that had not prepared them for college, and having few financial resources. When a student is the first in the family to attend college, a support system to help with things like setting realistic expectations, completing financial aid paperwork, or even filling out an application is often missing. Sometimes forms and essays are significant stumbling blocks that are difficult to overcome.

Students may come from a school system that set low expectations for them or delivered a curriculum that did not offer the skills or foundational courses necessary for college. With few financial resources, such students have to figure out how to earn money while also navigating an institutional system that is new to them. In other words, they may be working thirty or forty hours a week while carrying a full load of coursework.

Many have written about these challenges and how we need to design policies and procedures to help students overcome them. They approach the problem from a deficit perspective—describing the weaknesses in the system and the students' lack of resources. This approach has led to the development of multiple programs and strategies designed by educators to help underprepared students, and it has merit, although we believe it provides a limited view.

We wanted to explore the problem from a different and wider angle. We thought that by talking to students who had struggled and succeeded, we would be able to share a more comprehensive picture of what contributed to their

2

success. We would hear directly from the students about their experiences and what it took for them to achieve their goals.

We started by asking our colleagues from around the world who knew these students to recommend individuals willing to tell us their stories. Every student we reached out to was eager to talk to us. All of them readily agreed to meet with us via Skype and were excited that we cared enough to ask. They gave us permission to use their stories in written documents, on audiotapes, in presentations, on websites, and especially to share with other students. One student read a written statement to us at the conclusion of his interview that he had prepared for other students so that we could share it.

We continue to interview students, and so far we have interviewed students from Canada, South Africa, and the United States. Their struggles are similar, and their stories have many parallels. In chapter 2, we will introduce you to seven of these students, and we will carry their stories throughout the book.

What Did We Learn?

The student stories confirmed for us some of what we have seen throughout our years working with colleges and universities. We know, for example, that students who face challenges need a support system. There must be some type of institutional infrastructure. Whether it's a tutoring center or a center for a specialized population like first-generation students or veterans, students need a space where they feel comfortable asking questions and receiving academic and/ or personal support.

For instance, one student was an Iraqi war veteran attending community college. He talked about how important the veterans' center at his school was; it was there that he felt safe talking about his military experiences and receiving emotional support. Another student, who attended a small liberal arts college, talked about his school's center for first-generation students and how he would not have made it without its academic support. The staff there taught him how to write college-level papers, something he said was lacking at his high school.

These types of centers are significant, and that was confirmed across all the stories. What we learned and hadn't completely understood earlier, however, is how important it is for students to have specific individuals believe in them at a significant time in their life. This was the primary thread that was woven throughout the stories: all students identified at least one person who had encouraged them to persist in the face of overwhelming obstacles because of a strong belief in the student.

In chapter 2, you will hear Adam's story. He was in special education during his early school years, and when he arrived at the university, he was placed into all remedial classes. He was so devastated that he wanted to quit. He called his mom and, as he told us, "That's what made me really realize, you know, my mom believed in me, and the faculty believed in me, and I can do this, so I said, 'Okay.' Even though I'm personally hurting, I know I can arrive above this."

You will also hear about Jonah, who had six of his professors show up to a court hearing in order to speak on his behalf before a judge. He told us that one of the teachers said, "Man, he got in there; he buckled down; and he passed my class with an A ... He has a determination about himself." Jonah then added, "And hearing those good things just added more fuel to my fire inside to want to do well in school, to want to not please everybody but please myself. I want to make it not only in life but also in school."

From South Africa comes the story of two brothers, Patrick and Martin, who were the first in their family to attend university. Their families live in a township and are dependent on social bonds for survival. Martin told us, "We chose to go to college, reason being financial problem. We had financial difficulties in the family; like I said no one was working in the family. Our sisters, all the sisters, were pregnant, most of them, so we're like many. And our parents couldn't really focus on our education, reason being they were still having family or difficulties or having to provide for the family."

Having someone believe in you was clearly at the heart of all the stories. But as we continued to listen and connect all the dots, we found three significant factors that were also evident in all of them: The students exhibited persistence, emotional awareness, and self-efficacy. They didn't explicitly articulate these, but we clearly heard them as they described their experiences. We wove them together to create the Believe in You model that is described in chapter 6.

You may think these factors are nothing new. You're probably thinking, "Of course successful students have these characteristics." What we think is distinctive, however, is the way in which the integration of these factors and their direct link to having someone believe in you contribute to student success.

Why Listen?

While the stories we heard confirmed much of what we have experienced with our own students over the years, there was one area that caught us by surprise. We concluded each interview with four statements taken from Carol Dweck's book on mind-set (2006, 12):

- Your intelligence is something very basic about you that you can't change very much.
- You can learn new things, but you can't really change how intelligent you are.
- No matter how much intelligence you have, you can always change it quite a bit.
- You can always substantially change how intelligent you are.

We asked each student to tell us which statement he or she believed to be most true. Every student adamantly chose the final statement. Maybe this shouldn't have been a surprise, but these were students who had been held to low expectations for much of their early schooling; been placed in special education or remedial courses; and had every reason to feel less than self-confident about their ability to succeed in college.

Kristen, a student who had skipped much of high school and was suspended from college after a few semesters, told us, "So I actually had a professor when I was failing out of college … and she said a quote to me, and I actually have it tattooed on me because it's one of my favorite quotes … 'When you're green, you're growing; when you're ripe, you rot. And basically, to me, what it means is there's always room to grow, to learn, and to become better."

This belief in a growth mind-set reflects the spirit of the students whose stories we will share with you. We learned from listening to them and are more inspired than ever to continue our work with students who overcome significant challenges to reach their goals.

Ask Yourself

1. When was the last time I truly listened to someone's story?
2. What was the most powerful aspect of that story?
3. How did that story inspire me to take action? Why?

Chapter 2

Listening to the Voices

I just got fed up with the life I was living.

WE INVITE YOU to meet some of the remarkable students who so eagerly told their stories and gave us permission to share them with you. We introduce them here and revisit them throughout subsequent chapters by connecting their experiences to the Believe in You model that emerged from their stories.

You will hear about their challenges, fears, and ultimate successes. They come from community colleges, universities, and technical schools. We believe the way forward for those who face similar barriers is to build upon the strengths described in these stories. By analyzing the patterns found in these voices, we can develop principles for practice that lead to success.

Please listen carefully to the wisdom these students have to share.

Adam

Adam was diagnosed with a learning disability early in his life and received special education support to help him succeed. His motivation to succeed came from many sources, including his mother, who never graduated from high school but was a primary influence. "My mom always stressed that if you believe in yourself, put God first, and work really hard, you can achieve." Throughout his story, Adam emphasized the importance of family support. "My biggest success secret was to have that parent support."

Adam's mother fully supported his goal of attending college; however, many others didn't. He told us, "Most people didn't think that I would actually be able to go to college with ... having a learning disability. People didn't think that this would be possible to overcome."

With his mother's support and encouragement, Adam applied to and was accepted at a university in Louisiana. But his acceptance was conditional. He had to take remedial courses because of his placement-exam scores. After the initial elation of being accepted, he was deflated and discouraged. "Being placed in the remedial courses really hurt me at first; you know my pride was hurt, because I wasn't expecting this."

All too often, we hear of students becoming discouraged when placed into remedial/developmental courses. They lose confidence. They become demotivated. They fail to succeed. At first, Adam was no exception, but he rose above his disappointment. "I felt like giving up. I wanted to quit. I thought they made a mistake, that I didn't believe in myself ... my mom believed in me, and the faculty believed in me, and I can do this, so I said, 'Okay.' Even though I'm personally hurting, I know I can arrive above this."

He buckled down. He found strength in the voice of his mother. He refused to lose faith in his ability. As he explained, "[Taking] remedial classes ... was really to enhance me because they want to make sure I can be successful ... I had to change ... my thinking around to be more positive." Upon successful completion of the remedial coursework, Adam went on to take eighteen hours the next semester and earn a 3.8 grade point average.

Throughout his university years, others were there to boost his confidence, to encourage him through times of doubt, to strengthen his resolve to succeed, and to help him believe in himself. One adviser met Adam an hour before class and helped him understand a reading passage. A mathematics teacher encouraged Adam to come up to the front of the class and show others how to complete a problem. He said, "It gave me more confidence, too, because not only did I know it, but I was able to teach other students." His chemistry professor infused him with hope by saying, "'Okay, if you want to achieve it, I'm willing to work with you, but you have to be willing to put the work in too,' and I said, 'Yes.'"

Adam exceeded all the expectations of those who doubted him. His resolve to succeed coupled with the support of others who believed in him yielded amazing results. How did he describe his success? "My mom instilled us to really put God first, that's the first thing, my faith, and knowing that God has to come before me. Two was my mother's strong influence in us and raising her kids ... I had the faculty ... who really believed and knew there was a challenge but instead of running from it, they worked with me even harder."

After graduation, Adam went on to graduate school and ultimately earned a PhD in chemistry. When seeking employment after graduation, he remembers, "… my mother dreamed that one day her boys [would] be able to … wear a shirt and tie and carry a briefcase to work. That's why I always wear a shirt and tie, even for this interview, because I'm living my mother's dream."

Calvin

Learning came easily to Calvin. He earned good grades in high school and received a full basketball scholarship to the state university. Excelling in math and science, he majored in engineering. But coming from a small rural town, he found it difficult to adjust to life in a large college city. The distractions pulled Calvin away from his studies. He didn't regularly attend class. When not playing basketball, he spent time socializing, going to movies, and wandering around the mall. This was much more appealing than studying, and surely he would pull off good grades again without much effort.

He recalls, "I was always the guy who made good grades, so I kind of took it for granted that I would do it. In middle school, people said that it would be difficult in high school, and then I got to high school and that was easy, and so people said it would be difficult in college, and I thought to myself, *Well, it hasn't been hard yet, so why would it be hard now?*"

When he started getting poor grades, he panicked. "It just kind of freaked me out, to say the least. I was too ashamed to go get the proper help that I needed at the time. I wanted to sort it out on my own." He stopped going to class, flunked out, and lost his basketball scholarship. Keeping the failure a secret from his family, he was overcome with

11

shame: "I just didn't want to let them down, but I didn't want to tell them, even though that would've been the best thing to do because they love me and they want me to do the best. So I wasn't telling them, but I couldn't tell anybody else either, 'cause I was too ashamed to go to anyone else that I did not know, you know?"

Calvin stayed in the residence hall pretending everything was all right. He drove home on weekends to visit his father, who was seriously ill with cancer. The stress of academic failure and his ill father was taking its toll. When his father died, Calvin was overcome with remorse and shame. His secret of failure was secure until he was discovered illegally living in the residence hall and kicked out.

No longer a student, he found a job tutoring middle-school children in math and moved into an apartment near the campus. One day, the father of a boy he was tutoring pulled him aside and said, "Okay, what happened, because you are too smart not to be in college."

Calvin told him the story, "and he knew somebody, and that person actually knew a professor who could help me."

This professor became the changing force in Calvin's academic life. After meeting with her, Calvin reapplied and started college again. She was truly a highly motivating influence throughout Calvin's second try at the university. He said, "She really made me believe that I was at a different place in my life and that I would be fine. She really helped to calm me down. When she looked at my academic record, she just reinforced who I was. She reminded me of the things I had accomplished. She talked to me in a very calm manner, and she just gave me a perspective on things."

With her help, support, and guidance, Calvin reset his academic life. He regularly attended class. He learned and applied effective study strategies. He earned a perfect 4.0

grade point average. He became the first college graduate in his family and substituted overwhelming pride for the shame of his earlier experience. Calvin credits his turnaround to the people who helped him and believed in him.

Calvin also spoke of another professor: "She was so passionate, entertaining, but you could tell she really loved what she was doing, and I really learned in her class. I really did ... She's actually my model for being a teacher because she covered everything and ... she was friendly, but if you didn't care, you know, she didn't put up with any stuff either ... if you showed you didn't care then you're on your own, but if you showed you cared, she would go to the ends of the earth for you."

Today, Calvin is helping others as a middle school math and science teacher.

Jude

Jude faced more challenges than most. His father was murdered when he was a baby, and his mother gave him to his grandparents to raise. His grandparents died when he was twenty-one years old, and since then, Jude said, "It's just been me."

In high school, Jude lost motivation and was influenced by the "wrong people." As he described it, "I just fell into the wrong people and ended up dropping out, and really wasn't too concerned about my education ... Those were the type of people that cared more about themselves than anybody else. They'd say, 'Hey, let's skip school' or 'Let's go do this' or 'Let's not do that but let's go over here and drink' or 'Let's go over here to this party.'"

After dropping out of high school, Jude came to realize

the importance of the degree and studied to get his GED. He regained his motivation to succeed and subsequently entered a community college. With a strong resolve to receive a college degree, Jude actively sought help and soon found people at Tech to guide and support him. "I just got in touch with … instructors and said, 'Hey, I've been doing this on my own. I'm having a little trouble in this area right here. Would it be possible for me to talk to you?' And they didn't have one problem with it."

He continued, "I had no idea what I was getting in for whenever I wanted to become a student at a college, even community college. And I was just determined that I am going to succeed no matter what and, like you said, resources are a big part, even here at the college. You would not believe how the impact of your professors or your tutoring centers or even the library clerks here that will help you."

Positive influences were significant, but so was a negative one. Jude's brother was primarily absent throughout his life, but his influence was noteworthy: "Well, he influenced me a lot, believe it or not, because here I sit, and I see a man that's got three college degrees and he's got a degree of achievement and when he did have a job he was washing dishes at a restaurant. And then I'm thinking, why would you apply the time and do all that work for them degrees and do something that doesn't even apply to it? It just makes no sense, so I don't want to end up like that. I'm going to make sure that I'm going after what it is that I'm going to apply myself to. So he did help me see that."

Jude is a model for others striving to succeed and asked us to specifically share this statement with other students:

> For any student that's out there that has the ability to want to further their education and you're entering

a college, do not be afraid to ask for help and utilize every resource that you have available to you, because that's what they are there for. The tutoring centers are amazing people, your professors are the *best* probably possible *best* resource that you can have because they are very knowledgeable about what they are teaching, and do not be afraid to ask … the smartest and most intelligent people in this world didn't get where they are because they already knew what they know. They had to ask somebody, and they had to start exactly where we are, and I guarantee they had to ask too.

Jonah

Jonah was twenty-five years old when we interviewed him and had started community college at the age of twenty-two. He had attended three high schools before eventually graduating. As a college student, he worked two jobs in order to make ends meet and also enrolled in three to four courses per term.

Between high school and college, Jonah was convicted of two felonies. This put an end to his dream and scholarship opportunities to play basketball in college. Two schools had offered him scholarships, and he felt like he had let everybody down, including himself.

He served time in prison—two years in jail with ten years of probation. Upon his release, he went to work in a factory in order to pay his fines and court costs. After a few years, he was laid off and ended up living in his car. Eventually he moved to take care of a sick cousin who gave him a place to stay. He recalls thinking at that time, "I just made up my mind. I was sick and tired of being ... I feel like I was missing something, and that was my education."

At that point, Jonah returned home and enrolled in college. He says, "I took something negative and turned it into a positive. This is my fuel." He made it a point to get to know his teachers. One in particular convinced him to speak up in class and ask questions. He began to think of college as a way to concentrate on the positive and keep out of trouble. Jonah shared that it was the encouragement of the teachers and his classroom experiences that really made a difference for him.

His teachers told him, "We see a lot in you, Jonah. A lot of potential is in you." In the classroom, he shared his story with his peers: "If I can let them know anything about the streets and especially making the right decisions, you know, what goes on outside, don't let that change who you are. You can be anything you want to be. You can ... you can be a scientist. My major is chemistry. So I look at science as my getaway, and that's really, really helped me."

While in college, Jonah violated his probation and was back in jail for four weeks. During his court hearing, unbeknownst to him, six of his professors appeared in court to speak on his behalf. He choked up as he told us about their support for him in front of the judge who said, "By your GPA and your hard work in school, we're going to let you ... we're going to set you free." Among other things, one of his professors told the court that, "He has a determination about himself." Jonah told us that "hearing those good things just added more fuel to my fire inside to want to do well in school, to want to not please everybody but please myself."

When he first enrolled in college, Jonah felt "... kind of ashamed because of my age. I figured that this would be for a lot of students coming straight out of high school ... I think I was out of school for about four years, and I forgot everything that I had learned. Everything!" To help himself get past this fear, Jonah made it a point to get to know his professors, and they became role models for him.

For instance, one professor in particular shared with him how nervous she was before each class she taught. He watched how she overcame that nervousness and added it to his "repertoire and … style of speaking." When talking about her, he said, "I could talk to Dr. M. about anything. She … always has good advice … She's always been there for me, always from day one."

In addition to the teachers he named, Jonah also got to know "Minister Ray," a janitor at the school with whom he attends church and receives personal support. It is clear that Jonah recognized from the start how important having a support system would be to his success.

Jonah is doing his community service, and he tries hard to tell his story to the youth he works with. He talks about how he overcame his previous difficulties and that "I'm in college now pursuing my dreams and my major in chemistry and just praying to God that they will listen and take heed with what I have to say." He emphasizes how they shouldn't give up by emphasizing that they should "… set yourself away from the negative people that are around you … just focus in and don't give up when life throws you lemons. Make lemonade." Where he grew up, there were gangs and drugs. He doesn't choose to get involved in the community outside of his service because, as he says, "I left that alone years ago."

He talks about time management and how challenging it was for him at first. He needed to find time to focus on his work, so he decided to dedicate two hours a day to each course. Jonah went to the writing center, as he described himself as a "terrible writer." He says, "So I went to the writing center and before every paper just to revise ... I went there and they sit down and they worked with me for about two hours, and then I'd leave to go to work. And I took ... what they were saying, and I applied it ... I'd lock it in my head, and I applied it to every paper that I wrote." He goes on to say, "I had some pretty tough Comp [English composition] teachers. One teacher, he had gave me a D in Comp I, and I was not happy with that grade. I said, 'I know I can do better; I need to spend more time with writing.' So I retook Comp, and I passed with a B+."

Jonah has set educational goals for himself, and he passionately pursues them. He plans to stay in college until he is off probation, "... so I have plenty of time to reach any type of educational goal that I have set for myself ... Academically, I see ... there's a lot of obstacles. I know that as I reach ... the upper levels of chemistry, in math, that's going to take a lot of ... time to do all this and work at the same time and do community service. It's a lot on my plate."

When we asked Jonah for his perspective on the four statements related to mind-set, he responded, "You can always change ... you can always add." Your intelligence "[is] like a plant ... And as long as you're feeding it, it's going to grow. It's going to grow."

Kristen

Kristen was twenty-two years old when we interviewed her, and she had been raised primarily by her grandmother. Her mother was sixteen when she had Kristen and did not attend college. They lived together off and on, relocating often until Kristen was fourteen and went to live full-time with her grandmother. She had a younger sister who had a one-year old son and was about to graduate from high school.

She told us that she was "really ahead of the curve" in high school and got bored easily. As a result, she was always in trouble and finally "stopped doing what I needed to do because I just didn't care enough anymore." Kristen skipped school a lot and almost did not graduate, but she liked sports and had a coach who urged her to get the grades she needed to stay on the track team. This enabled her to graduate.

Kristen's grandmother was a software engineer and expected her to go to college. She recalls, "So I basically had no option. If I wanted a place to live, I had to go to college ... and I went there and I basically didn't go and I failed out and they put me on probation." She felt bad that she was disappointing her grandmother, so she went back.

As she tells it, "I went back, but I basically did the same thing ... I went for a little while ... and then I did the same thing. I stopped going, and I failed again ... So the first semester, I failed all four of the classes I was taking ... and then the second semester, when I went back, when I was on probation, I failed two of the four classes I was taking. So I ended up getting suspended." She shared that she simply wasn't ready for college and that she was going to please someone else, not herself.

As a result of her suspension, the school required that she take a semester off. During that time, Kristen worked at a gas station. That's when she realized, "I cannot do this for the rest of my life. I have to go to college ... I need a college degree. I can't be a manual laborer, minimum wage worker for the rest of my life. This is not me." She reapplied to the same school and joined the computer science department, following in her grandmother's footsteps.

Her grades were excellent, but she realized that this

was not the major for her, although it helped her identify her strengths. She got to know an adviser who helped her choose another major, where she also excelled. As she describes it, she went from a 0.0 GPA her first semester to a 3.51 following her return.

As she moved through the semesters, Kristen met advisers who "did everything ... to make it a really good experience for me." The first one "got me into all the classes that he could that he thought would be fun ... I felt really bad switching out of the department because of how hard he worked ... he was definitely the first one at Tech to make me want to be there and make me enjoy college. And then once I got into the math department, I decided that I wanted to tutor because I wanted to help people love math as much as I did, and so that was the next thing I did."

Kristen became close to her second faculty adviser, who got her involved in tutoring and then asked her to do undergraduate research during the summer. As Kristen says, "She has been one of the most fantastic faculty to work with because she's given me not only the opportunity to be an SI [supplemental instruction] leader, but also to do undergrad research, which has given me the opportunity to present at conferences ..."

When we asked Kristen to talk about what she would have done differently, she replied, "Honestly, I think it worked out well for me. I think the only reason that I am as successful as I am is because I failed the way that I did. I don't think I would be as driven as I am or as good of a tutor as I am had I not failed the way I did ... I'm also an academic coach, and what I do is I help freshmen and sophomores when they need help with things on campus ... I think part of the reason I'm so good at that is because I have failed and succeeded afterwards."

Kristen's educational goal is to take a year off after graduating to work and study for the actuary exams. She knows this will be difficult but she understands that "I've overcome a lot of hurdles, so as long as I can stay focused … I can succeed." She may go on to graduate school, but as she said, "If I make it to six figures in the future being an actuary and I love it, then I think maybe it won't be necessary unless my company asks me to."

Based on her experience, Kristen advises faculty to really take the time to get to know their students and figure out what would make them want to be in college. "You know, if I didn't have that first adviser when I came back actually take the time to make me want to be here, I don't know if I would still be at Tech. He's the reason that I really enjoyed being on this campus, and even though I didn't stay in the department … I still talk to him whenever I see him … He reminded me of how I could be successful."

Kristen concluded her story by affirming that she agreed one can substantially change how intelligent one is. She remembered a professor when she was failing who said something to her that she tattooed on herself because she found it so meaningful: *When you're green, you're growing; when you're ripe, you rot.* She explained that it means "… there's always room to grow, to learn, and to become better."

Patrick and Martin

Patrick and Martin are two brothers studying at a four-year university in South Africa. They grew up in a township and are the first in their family to attend university. They were twenty-four years old when we interviewed them. They shared their goal of becoming American doctors. At nineteen, they did not get accepted to the university, but they wanted to continue on their educational path and enrolled at a local college. Following their graduation, they were accepted to the university to "... pursue the dream that we had before ... We just wanted to study something that is related to medicine so that at the end we could get into the medicine field."

As they explained to us, "We are from very disadvantaged background of families whereby there was no one who *ever* managed to go to a college or university." Neither of their parents was working, and the family was dependent on social bonds. The family focus was not on the brothers' education; rather, it was to provide for their sisters who all had children.

One of their brothers had tried college but dropped out because of lack of finances. "That also discouraged us that we cannot get anywhere. But then we kept on motivating each other that no matter what, no matter the circumstances, we can always get to the dream ..." They had no financial support from their family, so they had to figure out how to continue their dream.

Patrick and Martin resolved that they would overcome the financial barrier by taking turns at the university. Martin told us, "I had to go to work or find a few jobs for one year. I was doing a one-year job in the retail marketing; whereas, he was studying. And by then, I could help him by buying him food ... I would help him to buy him stationaries ... As I was helping him with finances, he was helping me with finding me a space for a scholarship at school." They acknowledged how challenging this was and how hard they had to work in order to qualify for a scholarship that ultimately provided funding for them to continue.

They talked about what high school was like in the

township. "Most of the classrooms, they are very old classrooms, the ones that have been used by our own father ... the government couldn't provide enough teachers for enough students, especially for math and science. We didn't have a math or science teacher ... so we had to study math and science on our own. A library is like something we had never dreamt of. We never knew the first thing about a library ... It was only after we came to college and to university, that's when we knew that, 'Oh! There is something called the library!'"

Patrick and Martin believe that their family is "very honored" that they are attending the university. Their mother is especially proud, and "She always called us each and every day motivating us, telling us to study, telling us to really work hard ... She believes in us. She's really saying that *we*, as brothers, we are the ones to change the situation in the family; we are the ones to bring light into the family; we are the ones to motivate those young ones in the family that are coming after us."

When they talked about the faculty at the university, they spoke of them as family members. "Most of the lecturers, they are like my parents to me. I can go to them whenever I've got a problem or whenever I'm facing a challenge in a subject or in a particular module." They both fondly remembered one who was "like a mother. In her presence ... you feel free whenever you have a problem, whatever problem it might be, a bit initial problem, psychology type of problem ... if you're stressed; if you're confused; if there's something happening back at home, she is the right person ..."

They both spoke of how lecturers "must also put themselves in the shoes of the students. They must be able to teach the students not only academia, but also looking at the life of a student." They believe lecturers must be open, transparent, and approachable. Martin adds that most of the lecturers will make an appointment with you and "they will listen to your story ... to listen to what it is that you have to bring to the table." He continues, "The relationship between a student and lecturer must be like a parent and the child ... we need that somebody we can relate to as a parent, as a father figure, as a mother figure. Because now that we come from a different place. We need that someone we can talk to."

In addition to the faculty, the brothers both praised student mentors, who helped them establish relationships with their teachers. Martin said, "That's how I managed to pass my first year with flying color." Patrick became a mentor after his first year in order to help others overcome their challenges. The brothers also took a course entitled "Academic Life Module" that taught them about self-concept, communication, conflict management, emotional intelligence, and diversity. This was another key to their success as they learned "how to deal with life."

Martin offered this advice to students who are thinking about going to the university: "I would say to them that they must never give up, like there are so many students applying at the same time. Hundreds might get rejected; hundreds might get accepted, but for those who get rejected, they must never give up ... because you never know when will your door open."

Patrick added, "Regardless of where you come from, regardless of your background, regardless of race or culture, you can believe. You can make differences."

Martin and Patrick are continuing to pursue their goal of getting into a medical institute, although they recognize the challenges that lie ahead of them. They are optimistic and ended the interview with Martin saying, "So my plan B is that if I don't get into medical school, I'm going to become a nurse and then I will be waiting in the hospital until that opportunity arrives."

These stories represent just a small sample of all the students we interviewed. They do, however, vividly illustrate three major threads that are woven throughout all the stories. In the next few chapters, we will discuss these threads—persistence, emotional awareness, and self-efficacy—and how they interact to facilitate success, especially in the face of barriers.

Ask Yourself

1. What is the most powerful impact of these stories?
2. Which individual in this chapter stands out and why?
3. How do these stories inspire me to think differently about students who face challenges?

Chapter 3

Persistence

I've overcome a lot of hurdles, so as long
as I can stay focused, I can succeed.

ONE OF THE significant threads that runs through all of these stories is the concept of persistence. In spite of the challenges they faced and the setbacks they experienced, the students persisted in their determination to complete college. There were multiple triggers for this persistence. Jude, for example, had both positive and negative forces pushing him. He didn't want to end up like his brother washing dishes or the "wrong people" who had no goals beyond having a good time. He realized that education could lead him down a different path. Jonah lost a scholarship and spent time in prison, where he discovered he was "missing something." Kristen was suspended and spent a semester working at a gas station, after which she realized, "This is not me."

When we tried to pinpoint exactly what we mean by *persistence*, we recognized that the students all shared a cluster of common attitudes. This cluster included grit, resilience, and a growth mind-set, all closely related, and with overlapping dimensions. We will describe persistence through these shared attitudes. None of them should be viewed in isolation; rather, they are parts of a larger constellation of factors related to persistence and achievement.

Grit

Grit is specifically defined as an individual's passion for a long-term goal coupled with a powerful motivation to achieve an objective. Research shows that it is not positively correlated to IQ and that individual differences in grit can account for a significant variance in successful outcomes beyond IQ (Duckworth et al. 2007). Important variables related to grit include follow-through and continuous commitment to reaching a goal. These same variables are related to growth mind-set, emotional awareness, and self-efficacy.

Grit is related to stamina and the ability to overcome short-term failures or obstacles in order to continue working toward a long-term goal. Research indicates that grit can predict achievement in academic, vocational, and avocational domains. High school juniors in Chicago with a high degree of grit were more likely to graduate on time than their peers with less grit (Eskreis-Winkler et al. 2014).

This disposition was articulated across all the interviews. Adam was diagnosed with a learning disability early in his education and placed in special education classes. He said, "People didn't think that this would be possible to overcome." He added, "There's nothing that we cannot do if we believe in yourself and you're willing to work hard."

Adam graduated from the university and ultimately received his PhD.

Another relevant aspect of grit for student success is that individuals with grit are often able to continue to move forward after experiencing a barrier by "sprouting" new short-term goals that will lead them forward to the same long-term goal. Duckworth and Gross (2014) label these "lower-order goals" and contend that while those without grit might see them as unattainable, grittier individuals will find a way to achieve them.

One example from our stories comes from Calvin, who began as an engineering major at his university. After enduring several setbacks, he changed his major to general studies in order to move toward his ultimate goal of graduation. Another example comes from Patrick and Martin, brothers in South Africa. When it became clear that they did not have the financial resources to attend university together, they developed a strategy of taking turns. While one attended school, the other worked and provided the necessary resources, including finances, encouragement, and housing.

Resilience

Resilience is closely related to grit but is most useful when considered not as a fixed trait but "from a process of repeated interactions between a person and favorable features of the surrounding context in a person's life" (Gilligan 2004, 94). Research indicates that especially in young people, resilience is "highly dependent on other people and multiple systems of influence" (O'Dougherty Wright et al. 2013, 31). Once it was considered to be an innate characteristic, but today it is considered a developmental process dependent on the interactions between individuals and their environment. Some researchers (Masten 2001) suggest that everyone has the capacity for "self-righting." Masten refers to it as "ordinary magic" where most individuals who face adversity are able to arrive at "normative" outcomes.

Jonah is a good example of a student we interviewed who engaged in self-righting. He served two years in prison at the age of seventeen followed by ten years of probation. A few years after his release, he lost everything and went to live with a relative. After taking care of this sick relative for a while, he told us, "I feel like I was missing something, and that was my education. I just got fed up with the life I was living. I decided … the best way to make it through these ten years on probation was college … I took something negative and turned it into a positive. This is my fuel."

Resilience is often described in two-dimensional terms: an individual is exposed to adversity and adjusts to that adversity with positive outcomes (Luthar and Cicchetti 2000). Significant to this adjustment is the interplay between the number and strength of risk and protective factors in one's life (Garmezy 1993). These two factors are usually considered on three levels—individual, family, and environment—and they can increase or decrease over time depending on the interactions experienced.

There are multiple risk factors cited across the literature on resilience, including low socioeconomic level, inadequate resources, fragmented services, and low expectations (Williams et al. 2001). These risk factors are often reflected in underresourced educational institutions which Henderson and Milstein (2003) address by calling for schools to be "resiliency-fostering institutions." The most frequently cited protective factors for schools to provide include a caring and supportive environment, positive role models, educator-student relationships that build trust and respect, high expectations, meaningful participation, development of self-regulation, goal setting, and supportive peer groups (Esquivel, Doll, and Oades-Sese 2011; Seccombe 2002; Henderson and Milstein 2003; Barley, Apthrop, and Goodwin 2007; Brooks 2006; Williams and Bryan 2013).

From Jonah's story, we learn that his prison time was a significant risk factor. When he returned to school, however, he developed close relationships with his teachers. They continuously encouraged him and let him know how much potential he had. Soon after returning to school, another risk factor threatened to derail him again: he violated his probation and went back to prison for four weeks. At his court hearing, six of his college teachers appeared and testified about his determination and strong will to succeed. Hearing their support, the judge released him, and he returned to school. Of this experience, Jonah said, "Hearing those good things just added more fuel to my fire inside to want to do well in school, to want to not please everybody but please myself."

In addition to educational institutions (the environmental level), researchers have examined the influence of families. Williams and Bryan (2013) studied high-achieving African American students from low-income families with single mothers. They found that the protective factors present in these homes included verbal praise for high grades, high but realistic expectations, and a regular monitoring of the student's progress. These same students reported that the protective factors they experienced in school included a caring adult who knew them well; a peer network that valued education; high standards with learning that was relevant; and extracurricular activities.

We heard about the significance of family support from

several of our students. Patrick and Martin struggled in part because they were the first in their family to attend university. Their parents were unemployed and had little idea of what it meant to be in college. Their mother, however, called them every day and encouraged them to work hard. Patrick told us that "she really behind us … like we are motivated almost every day because of her, and we can see the reason why she's motivating us. She believes in us. She's really saying that *we*, as brothers, we are the ones to change the situation in the family; we are the ones to bring light into the family; we are the ones to motivate those young ones in the family that are coming after us."

Growth Mind-Set

The concept of mind-set is a good fit within this cluster of attitudes and has been shown to be a reliable predictor of academic performance. Dweck (2006) describes two types of mind-set. The first is *fixed*. Individuals with a fixed mind-set believe they have been endowed with an intelligence that does not change over time. They believe that no amount of effort will change what they consider to be innate. The second type is a *growth* mind-set. Those with a growth mind-set believe that their behavior can impact their intelligence and ability to achieve. They see intelligence as evolving over time through their efforts and strategic behavior.

This concept affected our students in different ways. Imagine what would have happened to Adam if he'd had a fixed mind-set. With a growth mind-set, he accepted his remedial course placement and moved beyond it. How about Martin and Patrick, who were initially turned away from the university? That rejection could have led them to believe they just weren't smart enough for college. Why did they push past that? Was it their attitude of grit? Resilience? How did these attitudes work together for these students?

On the other end of the spectrum, Calvin arrived at the university with a fixed mind-set. He had always succeeded academically with little effort and assumed that would continue at the university. Suddenly, this assumption was challenged when he received poor grades and flunked out. This led to feelings of shame and remorse. Gradually, through his subsequent experiences and effort, he developed a growth mind-set and "righted" himself. But suppose he hadn't received the guidance he needed for that development? His earlier fixed mind-set would have left him feeling inadequate and confused about his abilities.

Research conducted with low-income African American, Hispanic, and South Asian seventh graders demonstrated that students with a growth mind-set showed continuous improvement in math achievement, whereas those with a fixed mind-set did not (Blackwell, Trzesniewski, and Dweck 2007). The researchers concluded that the reason for their continued progress was related to three factors: they valued learning over simply looking smart; they considered effort a positive behavior; and they viewed failures as a reason to try new strategies.

All the participants in our study had a growth mind-set by the time we talked to them. The final component of the interview protocol asked each student to respond to the following four statements taken from Dweck (2006, 12):

1. Your intelligence is something very basic about you that you can't change very much.
2. You can learn new things, but you can't really change how intelligent you are.

3. No matter how much intelligence you have, you can always change it quite a bit.
4. You can always substantially change how intelligent you are.

Every one of the participants responded in the affirmative to the last statement. Not one demonstrated a tendency toward a fixed mind-set. Comments included the following from Jonah: "You can change … It's like a plant … as long as you're feeding it, it's going to grow." Calvin (whose mind-set changed) adds, "So I disagree that intelligence is fixed … You know, as intelligent as I came out to be in high school, I did not make it through college the first time. But even though I failed out, I regained myself and … made it happen."

Conclusion

This constellation of factors exerted a powerful effect on our students. It's difficult to imagine any of one of these factors being as significant alone; rather, they overlapped and together facilitated achievement. They interacted differently for each student, but they did interact to make a difference.

Ask Yourself

1. How important is the intersection of these factors?
2. What led to the development of a growth mind-set for Calvin?
3. How does this intersection work? Is it a linear progression?

Chapter 4

Emotional Awareness

> Even though I'm personally hurting, I
> know I can arrive above this.

EMOTIONS CONTRIBUTE TO learning in many ways. They affect the ability to remain focused and process information and can advance or impede learning success. Emotional intelligence lays a foundation for understanding why some students succeed and others do not. Here we use the terms *emotional intelligence* and *emotional awareness* interchangeably.

What did we hear throughout the narratives that demonstrated emotional awareness in the student stories? Statements like "I know I'm going to be able to get through it, that there's nothing that is going to really stop me from, you know ... accomplishing my goals" and "So I had to just buckle down and learn responsibility, and that's what helped me a lot."

The literature on emotional intelligence provides insight into the actions of the individuals in these stories. The term *emotional intelligence*, first used by Peter Salovey and John Mayer (1990), and Peter Salovey and David Pizarro (2003) refers to the ability to manage feelings and relationships. According to Daniel Goleman (1995), emotional intelligence involves self-awareness, self-management, social awareness, and social skills. Let's take a deeper look.

Self-Awareness

Self-aware individuals are able to read and understand their own emotions and recognize how these impact performance. For example, self-aware students know when they are feeling stressed or disturbed by personal difficulties. They are in touch with their feelings. They realize being stressed makes it difficult to concentrate and know they must find ways to reduce tension and adjust the tasks they are facing.

Self-aware people have realistic evaluations of their strengths and weaknesses. They know how to assess what they are able to do competently and when they need to overcome a limitation. Being aware of individual peak-performance times is part of becoming self-aware. For example, when you know you are most alert and productive in the morning, you may use this knowledge to effectively adjust your study time. If you know you work best in a quiet place without distractions, you avoid noisy, highly stimulating environments. If you are aware of your need to prepare well in advance of exams, you won't leave test review until the last minute.

Becoming self-aware requires openness to hearing and receiving feedback. Self-aware students seek feedback and use it to enhance self-knowledge. For example, feedback from others about how one listens and communicates is integrated into new and ever-evolving self-awareness.

Through introspection, individuals become aware of

their own needs, desires, habits, and failings. The more attention is centered on emotions and how they work, the more knowledge is gained about why things happen. The more knowledge about one's habits, the easier it is to change them. This knowledge leads to better adaptability and adjustment to change. With enhanced adaptability comes self-confidence and a strong positive sense of self-worth— all valued outcomes of becoming self-aware. Well-developed self-awareness leads to the next step of emotional awareness: self-management.

Self-Management

Self-management is characterized by self-control, trustworthiness, conscientiousness, adaptability, achievement orientation, and initiative (Goleman 1995, 2006). Let's see how each of these is exemplified in the stories.

Self-Control

Students typically face many temptations that can negatively affect success. Staying up late to party with friends instead of studying for tomorrow's exam; attending that all-important soccer match instead of going to class; or just chilling out and listening to music instead of joining a required study group can land a student in trouble. Repeatedly resisting an impulse to play over study surely has consequences. The ability to control disruptive emotions and impulses is critical to self-management.

Without exception, each of these stories is filled with evidence of the emotional awareness component of self-control. Jude described how he overcame the temptation to be with the "wrong people" who skipped classes to party. He found the willpower to resist the pull of partying, stay the course, and focus on his studies. Calvin lost control but regained it. Once he got back on track, he regularly attended classes. He didn't let others pull him away from the path to success. Jonah, after violating his probation, gained control and followed the rules that ultimately propelled him to graduate and give back to others.

Trustworthiness

A consistent display of honesty and integrity is a hallmark of self-management. Resisting the temptation to cheat on an exam or plagiarize a paper contributes to academic integrity and is a critical component of self-management. Less extreme but equally important is demonstrating reliability and trustworthiness in situations where others depend on you. Trustworthy students show up on time, actively participate on team projects, and follow through with promises.

Many of these students began their studies lacking trustworthiness. Calvin skipped classes, lied to his parents, and even lived illegally in the residence hall. None of these exhibits trustworthiness. Once he changed his path, however, trustworthiness became a central part of his character. He dedicated himself to helping others.

Conscientiousness

Students are loaded with multiple academic responsibilities. They must attend class, complete assignments, prepare for exams, write papers, and participate in study groups. And it doesn't end there. Many must hold down part-time or even full-time jobs and care for family members. Conscientious students know how to manage themselves and their many responsibilities. There is no effective self-management without conscientiousness.

Adaptability

Adapting successfully to ever-changing situations and environments is a key component of overcoming challenges and reaching goals. Flexibility and adaptability involve planning ahead, having alternative options, and persisting in the face of difficulties. All the students interviewed demonstrated this most important characteristic.

Adaptability was a challenge for these students. At first, it seemed the system had failed them. Adam resented being placed in remedial classes when he was confident he could succeed without them. He believed his placement in these classes was a mistake. Instead of fighting against the requirement, however, he reluctantly accepted the situation. It turned out to be a real advantage, as Adam gained both skill and confidence, propelling him to major success in subsequent terms. Jonah lost his focus with a probation violation only to regain his determination and adapt to this detour with the support of his professors.

Achievement Orientation

Achievement motivation—the need to meet realistic goals, receive feedback, and experience a sense of accomplishment—was expressed by all the students. Realistic goal setting wasn't present at the beginning. Calvin expected his college studies to be like high school, so he didn't set realistic study goals. At first, Jonah overloaded his time at work and course schedule, not realizing the amount of studying required. Kristen underestimated the importance of achieving a goal based on her own interests.

Only after failures did these students become open to receiving feedback and adjusting expectations to set realistic goals. Once they turned the corner and experienced success, the sense of accomplishment was overwhelmingly positive for all of them. Achievement motivation continued to guide them to graduation and beyond. Jonah shared his experience of getting a D in English composition. "I was not happy with that grade. I know I can do better, so I retook Comp, and I passed with a B+."

Initiative

Initiative, or the ability to assess and begin things independently, is critical for self-management. On the rebound after failures, these students displayed an amazing degree of initiative. Patrick and Martin demonstrated initiative with their well-developed plan to alternate enrollment in the university. While one brother studied, the other worked to help financially. They accomplished their goals by assessing what it took to get it done and taking the initiative to create a plan to succeed.

Jonah took the initiative to reorganize his study plan and devote two hours a day to studying for each course. He sought help on his own in the writing center. His initiative continued in his community service work, where he shared his struggles to help others.

Social Awareness and Social Skills

The socially aware individual is empathetic and senses others' emotions while taking an interest in their concerns. In addition, being socially aware involves building networks and relationships. Social awareness leads to the development of such social skills as effective communication, conflict management, teamwork, collaboration, and the drive to help others. Many of the students in this study expressed a desire to help others and did so through tutoring and mentoring activities. Some got involved in campus organizations that helped them become more connected to the institution while serving others.

Adjusting to changes and overcoming obstacles is critical to the development of emotional intelligence. The individuals in this study all displayed an ability to adapt and adjust, so their challenges ultimately became opportunities. The connection between emotional intelligence and learning success is evident throughout this study. Building bonds and cultivating and maintaining relationships is particularly present.

All the students developed and maintained relationships with significant others who recognized their potential and supported their success. These helpers set boundaries within a supportive environment, had high expectations of the students, provided validation of their accomplishments, and helped influence positive emotions leading to success.

Social skills, or the drive to help and develop others, is a key component of emotional awareness. The students we interviewed evidenced this most effectively as they continued past graduation to pursue experiences in teaching and the helping professions. Calvin is giving back to others through his dedication as a teacher. Adam is now teaching college students and is keenly aware of how his own struggles inform his work as an educator. Kristen contributed her expertise as a tutor, helping other students overcome challenges similar to those she faced. Giving back to others is evident in these stories and underscores the importance of emotional awareness on the path to success.

Ask Yourself

1. What component of emotional awareness is most important for student success?
2. How do failures contribute to the development of emotional awareness?
3. How did emotional awareness impact my own success as a learner, and what triggered it?

Chapter 5

Self-Efficacy

> I can relate to the kids that are doing well and are
> used to making As 'cause I've been that guy, and I
> can relate to the kids that, you know, are struggling
> at studies because I've been that guy too.

SELF-EFFICACY IS BELIEF in one's likelihood of successfully completing a specific task. It is the belief that one's actions will affect change. This is clearly connected to growth mind-set, grit, and resilience. These beliefs are critical to overcoming challenges and succeeding academically.

The importance of self-efficacy is supported by research. Individuals with higher self-efficacy beliefs tend to be more motivated and successful at a given task. Self-efficacy has also been associated with the use of cognitive strategies where self-efficacy perceptions predict achievement over and above actual ability levels (Pintrich and De Groot 1990, Bertrando 2014).

Albert Bandura's research asserts that self-efficacy is the major component of effort, persistence, and goal setting. According to Bandura (1986), there are four determinants of self-efficacy beliefs: personal experiences; vicarious experiences; verbal messages and social persuasion; and physiological states. Let's take a closer look at exactly how self-efficacy beliefs develop and contribute to student success.

Personal Experiences

Positive outcomes raise self-efficacy beliefs, whereas negative outcomes lower them. Calvin dropped out of college and began tutoring to make ends meet. The performance of the students he tutored significantly improved. As a result, the belief in his own ability to be academically successful increased. When he was praised by the father of one of his students, his self-efficacy beliefs were further enhanced. This experience helped him decide to return to college and complete his degree.

When Adam was able to show his peers how to solve complicated problems, his self-efficacy zoomed. "In mathematics, the teacher saw I was good so what he did, he'd have me come up to [the] front of the board and teach the other students; therefore, it gave me more confidence too, because not only did I know it, but I was able to teach other students."

When Jonah's teachers showed up in court to support him and testify that he deserved leniency for violating probation, his self-efficacy soared. "I had violated my probation, and I was in jail for four weeks, and upon my court hearing—I didn't know anything about this—but about six of my professors showed up to court and they spoke on my behalf. And the things they had to say was ... it brought me to tears." These powerful personal experiences feed academic self-efficacy beliefs.

Vicarious Experiences

Self-efficacy beliefs are also formed as individuals make social comparisons with others similar to themselves. The students in this study gave many examples of vicarious experiences leading to higher self-efficacy beliefs.

Jude saw his brother earn a college degree but end up in trouble and become incarcerated. He was determined not to end up like his brother. Through social comparison, Jude gained positive self-efficacy and remained dedicated to achieving his goals.

Kristen became a research assistant where she was able to work with someone who became a role model. She recounts having the opportunity to travel and present at conferences alongside this person, where she gained significant self-efficacy in her ability to perform in her chosen field.

Patrick and Martin had very rich mentoring experiences. "So the university hired mentors to mentor their students who are not working. So they came, and then they motivated me. They established a relationship between me and my lecturer, and then that's how I managed to pass my first year with flying color." Vicarious experiences with mentors were a major influence on these young men as they struggled to succeed against some very significant odds.

Verbal Messages and Social Persuasion

What we say to our students and how we communicate with them is critical to the development of their self-efficacy beliefs. Honest and supportive feedback is central to promoting positive self-efficacy. Verbal messages and social persuasion are strong influences and serve to either boost or deflate self-efficacy beliefs. We heard so many examples in these stories.

When Adam connected with his chemistry teacher, he benefitted from her praise and encouragement along with specific suggestions for overcoming barriers to academic success. Receiving praise and encouragement helped form positive beliefs to combat the discouragement and weakened beliefs from negative messages like the ones Adam received upon entering college. He was discouraged from pursuing a degree in science when an academic adviser said, "'I don't think you really … I don't think you have the qualifications for it.' … He didn't even want to talk to me, just brushed me off." Fortunately, for Adam, the positive messages prevailed, and with enhanced self-efficacy, he pursued and attained a doctoral degree in chemistry.

Martin's self-efficacy beliefs were developed and strengthened when he approached teachers and asked questions without fear. "If I can't approach you, I cannot talk to you. And if I can't talk to you, I will never understand you. And you'll never hear my story. I'll never be open to you. I'll never tell you my problem, if you're not approachable."

Jonah overcame feelings of doubt and gained positive self-efficacy beliefs as his teachers praised him. "My teachers … they come to me and they always got encouraging things to say and they … they really … they told me, 'We see a lot in you, Jonah, a lot of potential is in you.'"

Kristen talked about her adviser: "He did everything he could to make it a really good experience for me. He wanted to so badly for me to stay in the department, and so he had me work on projects with him, and he got me into all the classes that he could that he thought would be fun." Even though she changed majors, his words continued to motivate her to stay focused and believe in herself.

Physiological States

When an individual is in a state of anxiety or stress, self-efficacy beliefs are weakened. During his first effort at college, Calvin was faced with the debilitating illness of his father, who subsequently died. With increased stress and anxiety, he stopped attending classes and lost his focus and will to learn. His self-efficacy plummeted, and he kept his academic failure a secret from everyone. This created more stress, basically paralyzing him in his attempt to succeed.

Jonah's prison experience and the anxiety associated with violating his probation came close to debilitating him and weakening progress toward his academic goals. Patrick and Martin faced basic physiological challenges, as they needed to earn money for shelter and food not only for themselves but for their family as well.

Physiological stress is a significant contributor to deflating self-efficacy beliefs. Meeting basic needs for health, shelter, and safety are a necessary foundation for personal growth, including the development of self-efficacy beliefs.

Recent research in higher education lends support to the importance of self-efficacy. Students in science courses in a large public college in New York were found to have self-efficacy beliefs that changed over the course of the semester. These changes positively predicted final course grades (Di Benedettoa and Bembenutty 2013). Another study examined self-efficacy beliefs of students in a college developmental reading course. The findings indicated that mastery experiences were the most influential on reading self-confidence (Cantrell et al. 2013). A review of sixty-four articles on self-efficacy published since 2000 shows there is a strong association between self-efficacy beliefs and learning outcomes (Bartimote-Aufflick et al. 2015).

Ask Yourself

1. What verbal messages do I give students that affect self-efficacy beliefs?
2. How do my own self-efficacy beliefs influence my behavior?
3. How do self-efficacy beliefs change?

Chapter 6

An Integrated Model

You must believe that you can make a difference.

T HE BELIEVE IN You model emerged from the stories that came directly from students who faced challenges yet went on to achieve academic success and meet their goals.

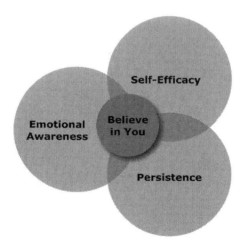

The primary factors correlated with student success that we have described—persistence, self-efficacy, and emotional awareness—are not new. They have traditionally been associated with success, but the significance of this model is the way in which they intersect and relate to the central phenomenon of having someone "believe in you." Of the students we talked to, 100 percent clearly articulated, with no prompt, the significance of having someone believe in them at a crucial time in their lives.

Sometimes this belief came from a parent: "My biggest success secret was to have that parent support." Sometimes it came from a teacher's tough love: "Her hard work and discipline in helping me ensured me that I was able to do well." And sometimes it came from a community member who asked the right question at the right time: "Okay, what happened, because you are too smart not to be in college."

Knowing that someone believed in them was closely aligned with the other factors we heard from the students. For example, Adam was diagnosed very early in life with a learning disability. He shared that "my mom believed in me, and the faculty believed in me." He persisted toward his ultimate goal even though, as he told us, when he was placed into remedial classes, "my pride was hurt." Despite the initial diagnosis of dyslexia, he learned to develop a growth mind-set and self-efficacy from teachers who would "have me come up to [the] front of the board and teach the other students." He shared with us that "it's just all how hard you're willing to work." He came to believe in himself and have confidence that he could achieve his goal of receiving a PhD, which he did.

Patrick and Martin received a daily phone call from their mother, who did not have a formal education, encouraging them to continue their studies. They live in South Africa, and their original goal was to become American doctors, but they did not get accepted to the university and did not have the finances to pursue other options. They displayed grit by adjusting their goals and beginning their studies in a field related to medicine. Martin told us, "My plan B is that if I don't get into medical school, I'm going to become a nurse, and then I will be waiting in the hospital until that opportunity arrives."

It also became clear from the stories that when the students became more emotionally aware, they began to take responsibility for their success. Calvin had been successful throughout high school but flunked out of college. He told us that he "questioned my abilities after I ... flunked out" and "I kind of panicked and didn't act on the situation." He was also "too ashamed to go get the proper help." He dropped out completely when he lost his scholarship but was encouraged to return by coworkers who believed in him. He managed to return to school, where he met instructors who "restored my confidence." He no longer felt ashamed to ask for help; he came to realize that he could not do it on his own.

The student stories suggest that there are strong correlations among the factors identified in this integrated model. We do not suggest a direct cause and effect, but we do believe there are strong interaction effects among the factors of persistence, self-efficacy, and emotional awareness that, when connected to having someone believe in you, help students achieve their academic goals.

Our model is a socio-emotional approach to learning, and we recommend that it be intentionally integrated across all learning environments through a developmental lens for *all* students. We must recognize the impact of students' personal backgrounds and the risk factors they have encountered in their lives, but we cannot set rigid expectations around them. Too often, educators are looking for *causes* of both failure and success rather than seeking *correlations*, and too frequently the factors we are describing here are associated with having a bias against students from challenging environments.

Learning from our students, let's facilitate the development of a growth mind-set by emphasizing effort through our feedback; help students become more resilient by providing a more protective (supportive) environment; increase self-efficacy by giving students a chance to succeed; and enable students to develop grit by helping them become aware of their passions and finding ways to set goals related to those.

Implications for Practice

We've heard the stories. We've read the research and examined underlying theoretical foundations. Based on all of this, we recommend five principles for practice. For each principle, we suggest strategies that can facilitate its implementation. Although we link the strategies to specific principles for the sake of clarity, the student interviews indicate that they are meaningful as part of a whole rather than as discrete approaches. The data suggest that we view them holistically and integrate them across all environments.

Principles and Strategies

1. Facilitate a growth mind-set.

Research indicates that approaching learning with a growth mind-set can increase motivation and enhance achievement (Haimovitz and Corpus 2011). Students with fixed mind-sets believe that there is not much they can do to change their performance, whereas those with a growth mind-set believe that through their efforts, they can enhance their current capabilities. What can we do to encourage a growth mind-set approach?

First, we can address the concept of mind-set directly with our students. By asking them to respond to the four statements that we presented to our interviewees, we are making them aware of the differences. Once they are aware of their own self-beliefs, we can facilitate a discussion around the probable outcomes of the two approaches. By providing examples from our own personal experiences and also asking students to share theirs, we can help those with a fixed mind-set reflect and begin to revise their thinking.

For example, we could use the story of Adam, who was diagnosed with a learning disability early in his educational career and put into special education classes. Those around him had low expectations for his college success. Adam, however, had a growth mind-set. He worked hard to overcome his disability and eventually earned his PhD. Another example is Jonah's story about the professor who shared how nervous she was before each class she taught. She became a model for him as he observed how she overcame her nervousness. He then put her strategies into use himself.

Secondly, we can provide feedback that encourages persistence and practice. Based on Dweck's work (2006), we should avoid complimenting students simply for their intelligence or native ability. This confirms for them that intelligence is fixed and that if they do not have the innate ability, there is little they can do. We need to find ways to assign value to persistence and practice. We can encourage students to persist in their efforts by requiring drafts of projects. For instance, for a first draft, we do not assign a grade; rather, we provide comments based on the strengths we find in the work and urge students to continue with a second draft. Once they are ready to submit the final project, we can help them see their improvement and understand that it was the result of hard work, not innate ability.

Third, and closely related to the previous strategy, we need to gain the trust of our students through our comments on their work. It is easy to be judgmental when grading papers, but that can contribute to an already fixed mind-set (Dweck 2006). By limiting comments to overall patterns, not each discrete error, and finding strengths throughout a paper, we demonstrate that we are not judging; rather, we are working along with students to make their work better.

2. Create an emotionally supportive environment.

Creating an emotionally supportive environment involves a number of very specific and intentional strategies. First among them is being sure to affirm the accomplishments of students without emphasizing competition. Competition can lead to situations where students hesitate to participate. Research shows that academic performance improves when mastery goals (personal growth and development) are emphasized over performance goals that involve comparison with others (Roeser, Eccles, and Sameroff 2000).

Emotionally supportive learning environments involve positive interactions that include respect, empathy, and encouragement for learning without fear of humiliation. Students in emotionally supportive environments are more likely to be comfortable taking risks without fear of ridicule or embarrassment. In the case of Adam, the chemistry professor was an important source of emotional support. She met with him regularly and provided continual encouragement. She helped him persevere in the face of challenges and provided a safe place where he could begin to believe in himself.

Focused and detailed positive feedback for well-deserved achievements is a critical component of emotionally supportive environments. High expectations along with support and encouragement in noncompetitive ways promote learning success. Calvin questioned himself as he voiced, "Maybe I'm not as smart as I think I am." His confidence waned. He began to lose motivation until a supportive faculty member entered his life. "She just reinforced who I was. She reminded me of the things I had accomplished." Her focused and detailed feedback became the basis for his renewed self-belief.

Jonah received significant encouragement from his teachers. He credits encouraging teachers with his drive to succeed and his determination not to give up. This feedback contributed to strengthening his confidence and self-belief. The importance of feedback cannot be ignored and is a critical element in the success of the students in this study (Wiggins 2012).

Learning situations that emphasize self-awareness are emotionally supportive. Modeling self-reflection and self-awareness is one way to help students become more self-aware, identify their feelings, and gain control over negative thoughts. Discussing both positive and negative feelings helps students become more comfortable in challenging situations so they can use positive thoughts to overcome difficulties. This was a significant factor for Kristen, who did not have meaningful goals until she met a faculty member who helped her develop enthusiasm for learning and understand how education could build on her strengths.

Promoting honesty and integrity is also essential in an emotionally supportive environment. Explicitly sharing guidelines and expectations is important, as is agreement on consequences for lack of integrity. Examples of dishonesty and failure of integrity can be helpful to further explain this aspect of an emotionally supportive environment.

Listening actively and communicating in a clear and unambiguous manner is essential. Opportunities to be heard in a nonjudgmental way are less threatening and more conducive to learning success (Bond 2012). Patrick and Martin referred to their faculty as family members. Martin said about one professor, "She's like a mother. In her presence ... you feel free whenever you have a problem, whatever problem it might be ..."

3. Promote realistic self-efficacy beliefs in each student.

One of the most effective ways to promote realistic self-efficacy beliefs is to help students develop a specific learning strategy and then have them describe it through the detailed steps involved (Ambrose and Bridges 2010). As the students use the strategy, they note their progress verbally or in writing. In this way, they are in touch with their success along the way. Instructors must be sure to compare student performance to goals set and not to the performance of others. In this way, self-efficacy is built around the accomplishment of goals and not through competition.

Realistic self-efficacy beliefs are developed when students are given choices and not required to rigidly adhere to task requirements. For example, students may be allowed to choose among a set of different assignment due dates or to select from a variety of different ways to complete a requirement. In this way, students gain autonomy leading to self-efficacy in the learning process.

Targeted feedback is feedback that specifically compares current performance to past performance and emphasizes effort and not comparison with others. Frequent and targeted feedback is very helpful in creating realistic self-efficacy beliefs (Zimmerman and Schunk 2013).

The use of peer models is also very effective. When students are faced with a task and see peers successfully performing it, they are more likely to persist. Seeing peers struggle and overcome obstacles also helps develop realistic self-efficacy beliefs. Patrick talked about how important his student mentors were as he learned how to establish relationships with his teachers. These peers were so significant to him that he became a mentor himself in order to help others overcome their challenges.

Encourage students to try. Give them support by saying, "I know this may seem difficult, but if you proceed in small steps, I know you can do it" and "Break up the task into smaller parts so it won't seem overwhelming." These statements go a long way to keeping students motivated with realistic self-efficacy beliefs.

Finally, make the most of students' interests and tie assignments in to them. For example, in a history course, allow students to connect their own family heritage to an era or to research sports as they occurred in that time period. The more interested students are, the more they are likely to persist and have self-efficacy beliefs that lead to successful learning (Zimmerman and Schunk 2013).

4. Develop student grit through alignment of short- and long-term goals.

The development of grittiness often depends on an individual's ability to adapt along the way to achieving long-term goals (Stoltz 2014). Frequently, in order to attain the goal of college graduation, for example, one must be willing to adjust a short-term goal. Patrick and Martin are two excellent examples of this strategy. Originally, they wanted to go to medical school and attend school together. Their willingness to shift their goals allowed them to continue on the path to graduation. They both adapted their short-term goals by taking turns attending school in order to support each other and studying in a health field related to medicine but not medical school. They are still headed toward college graduation. How can we help others to make these short-term adjustments?

One way to begin a discussion with students about grit is to ask them to respond to the "Grit Scale." This was developed by Duckworth et al. (2007) and contains twelve items that will prompt self-reflection and discussion. Items include, "I have overcome setbacks to conquer an important challenge," "Setbacks don't discourage me," and "I become interested in new pursuits every few months." Once the students have completed it and rated themselves in terms of grittiness, the discussion can begin.

This can be one component of a unit on achieving long-term goals. Once the students begin sharing their own experiences, it may be helpful to invite others to the discussion. Alumni of the program, student coaches, or staff members can share their own stories. At the conclusion, students can complete an action plan that aligns short-term goals with long-term goals.

Students can become discouraged when a short-term goal becomes an obstacle. For instance, if a student wants to become an engineer but fails the first physics course, how can we help that student overcome this barrier without giving up the long-term goal? We can certainly recommend working with a tutor or learning center to identify and strengthen concepts that were particularly challenging. We could also advise the student to take the course at a time when she won't be taking any other course in order to focus only on physics. These options will cause the student to take additional time to reach the ultimate goal and may also ensure that she reaches it.

We can help students develop flowcharts that visually show the pathways from short-term to long-term goals. Flowcharts include options if one path doesn't work; students will need to think about creating alternatives and building them into the chart. By engaging in this activity, they will be forced to create different pathways all leading to the same end.

5. Strengthen protective factors to increase student resilience.

Resiliency theory and research lead us to think about the interaction of the protective factors a student encounters versus the number of risk factors present in the environment. Many of our students come to us with multiple risk factors, so how can we ensure a resiliency-fostering learning environment? What protective factors can we offer?

We heard from all the students we interviewed that having a close relationship with a teacher or staff member contributed significantly to their successes. These relationships led to their feeling that someone believed in them and held them to high standards. The research on resiliency provides a strong foundation for this (Esquivel, Doll, and Oades-Sese 2011).

One way to develop a trusting relationship with students is to make time for them on an individual or small-group basis. When we hold our office hours at student-friendly times, we increase the likelihood that students will take advantage of the opportunity. When they do, it gives us an opportunity to get to know them beyond the classroom. These are the times when we can best provide advice, demonstrate tough love, and tell them we believe in them. We listen to their individual stories and gain more insight into their backgrounds, personal interests, and long-term goals. Once we learn about students' personal interests and goals, we can design assignments that will seem more relevant to them. If we match those to high standards, we can foster their resilience.

We can encourage the formation of peer-group interactions by assigning projects that require collaboration and working as a team. If we know something about our students' backgrounds and interests, we can construct teams that will embrace a supportive and encouraging dynamic based on its members. For example, one of the students we interviewed talked about how important it was for him to get to know others who shared his values and goals. Together, students can motivate each other.

As we are getting to know our students and creating a climate of trust, we must continue to articulate high standards and expectations. Our courses must be rigorous. A significant element of a difficult course is to provide the scaffolding (means of support) students need to succeed. The scaffolding can include tutors dedicated to the course, after-class instructional support, or online advice as needed. We must tell them multiple times that we believe in them and find the strengths they bring before identifying their weaknesses. They probably already know all about the latter.

Ask Yourself

1. What cluster of factors was most significant to Martin and Patrick when they adjusted their long-term goal?
2. How did developing emotional self-awareness contribute to Calvin's success?
3. What had the biggest impact on Adam's ability to develop a growth mind-set?
4. Do I believe any of these factors represent a bias against students from challenging environments?

Chapter 7

Future Implications

W E'VE HEARD THE stories, analyzed the content, and presented the Believe in You model. We've seen the significance of one individual helping and inspiring another—of believing in the power of one person to enhance the learning and success of a fellow human being. How is this knowledge employed in practice? We suggest using a systems approach to integrate and apply what we've learned to better meet the needs of students.

A systems approach is student-centered, contains shared values and behavioral norms, emphasizes collaboration across units, and is organizationally transparent and authentic. This approach promotes interaction among all constituents, helps guide decision-making, addresses unforeseen events, and ensures evaluation to sustain progress toward goals.

Kotter's system approach (2012) is one way to create a vibrant and effective learning culture. It begins by establishing a sense of urgency where potential threats are identified, opportunities are examined, honest discussions take place, and support is gained from others.

A sense of urgency can be inspired by many things, including declining student enrollment, limited financial aid, more students failing a particular course, reduced use of the library, or less funding for resources. These circumstances become potential threats to the sustainability of the learning enterprise.

Once urgency is established and discussed, a guiding coalition is formed where participants from diverse units work together to explore options for addressing the threats. The coalition works to develop a vision and a strategy to achieve it. For example, a reduction in resources may lead to shared resources among units or departments. Enhanced tutoring services and educational support may be connected to courses where students are failing. Library hours may be changed or increased to accommodate more student use.

The vision is communicated clearly and widely. When resources must be shared, plans for equal distribution are developed and communicated to reduce anxiety and distrust. The guiding coalition prepares a communication plan and openly shares information to keep everyone involved in the change.

Obstacles are identified, and plans are developed to overcome them. When financial aid is limited, alternate funding sources are explored. When more students fail, placement exams are reexamined, curricula are reviewed, and instructional delivery methods are analyzed. Admissions criteria and recruiting efforts are reviewed when student enrollment declines. Do recruitment efforts need to be refocused? Are recruitment methods in need of modification and diversification?

As the learning culture evolves, short-term wins are generated to demonstrate progress. For example, when more is done with less, departments are recognized and acknowledged for successfully using shared resources. When new recruiting efforts result in increased student enrollment, admissions personnel are highlighted. Every win is analyzed and goals are set to build momentum. Ideas are kept fresh and new leaders are brought into the process.

Finally, the learning culture is firmly anchored and considered a norm within the values of the institution. Winning changes such as extended library hours, revised curricula, modified placement testing, or team-teaching methods are considered standard and expected across the institution.

A systems approach stresses the interactive nature of learning and the multiple factors contributing to student success. It underscores the importance of going beyond the classroom to the whole organizational culture, from campus recruiter to admissions counselor, academic adviser, faculty member, cafeteria staff, and building maintenance personnel.

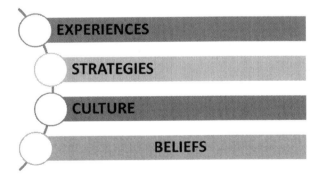

In a systems approach, beliefs form the foundation for all that follows. In these stories, we learn that students succeed when they persist, are emotionally aware, and have positive self-efficacy beliefs. Effective learning environments are constructed so that these dimensions are central to the overall culture, strategies advance each component, and experiences are provided to sustain successful learning and social-emotional development.

What Does This Learning Culture Look Like?

A Believe in You learning culture is characterized by considering the whole student environment and not just academic competence. It is apparent from the first point of contact, on the institutional website, and in all communications to the wider community. In this culture, the two units of student affairs and academic affairs are partners working together and providing support for the learning process. Collaboration among faculty and student affairs staff is the norm. The counseling center, advising office, enrollment management, library, and learning assistance center are physically located in close proximity to classroom instruction.

Administrators across all divisions meet regularly with each other, strategic planning meetings are conducted jointly, and professional development opportunities are offered simultaneously to both groups. Conference attendance and presentations are jointly experienced and shared.

Faculty members participate with all staff in orientation and advising activities. Research on student learning and development is conducted by both academic and student affairs professionals, and the research results are used to inform instructional approaches.

Cocurricular experiences that enhance and complement the curriculum are integral to the culture. For example, service-learning opportunities are provided within the context of specific course offerings. Academic course credit may be given for experiential, out-of-classroom learning experiences.

Preparation of grant proposals for the advancement of learning outcomes is a shared responsibility. Search committees for all positions consist of members from both academic and student affairs. Faculty members may conduct their office hours in different locations on campus. As Keeling (2006) states: "Given our current understanding of learning, collaboration between faculty and student affairs educators is not simply an intelligent option; it is a core requirement for the effective development and achievement of desired student learning outcomes."

How Are "Believe in You" Strategies Integrated into the Culture?

Persistence, emotional awareness, and self-efficacy are promoted and enhanced with specific learning strategies based on the five principles mentioned in the previous chapter and further outlined in appendix A. How are these strategies integrated in the Believe in You learning culture and translated into student experiences?

Persistence

In these stories, the students persisted against many odds, including family illness, financial distress, academic failure, and lack of adequate academic readiness. A learning culture that promotes persistence must recognize potential challenges and barriers and be ready to adjust the climate to help students overcome them.

Persistence is promoted by providing options for students who are working and have family obligations. These options include evening and weekend classes; extended library, counseling, and learning-assistance hours; and opportunities for advising by telephone or electronic communication.

Persistence is also advanced when students are given a choice about how to complete assignments and demonstrate learning. This learning culture allows students to select from a menu of choices in their courses so that assessment is not always based on tests and exams.

Principle 1, "Facilitate a growth mind-set," directly connects to persistence. In this learning culture, students assess their progress step by step. They are encouraged to determine how to improve their performance with focused effort and time on task.

Principle 4, "Develop grit through alignment of short- and long-term goals," is evident in all learning endeavors. Meetings with advisers to determine academic progress, discussions with teachers addressing assignment completion and course requirements, and regular sessions focusing on progress toward graduation all advance this principle.

Emotional Awareness

Opportunities for helping students enhance their emotional awareness occur everywhere in the learning culture—in the classroom, on the athletic field, in student organizations, during advising sessions, and in cocurricular activities. Self-awareness, self-management, and social awareness are developed through leadership training seminars, personal growth workshops, participating on search committees, and inclusion in strategic planning endeavors.

In these student stories, self-awareness was increased through supportive contact with significant others. You will remember that Calvin became more self-aware when he was recognized by the father of a student he was tutoring. Adam increased his self-awareness with opportunities to help others in his remedial classes.

We heard about tutoring experiences significantly increasing self-management and social awareness. Becoming a tutor and helping others succeed was a recurring experience leading to enhanced emotional awareness. An effective learning culture provides space for students to help each other and grow emotionally.

Principle 2, "Create an emotionally supportive environment," contains strategies for helping students develop their emotional well-being.

Principle 5, "Strengthen protective factors to increase student resilience," is central to creating an environment that enhances emotional awareness. In this learning culture, students under stress know where they can go to get relief. All campus personnel—including administrators, faculty, student development professionals, and maintenance staff—are trained to recognize students under stress and know how to guide them to the appropriate resources.

Self-Efficacy

We know that positive self-efficacy beliefs lead to success, while negative ones impede progress. In this learning culture, positive beliefs are promoted through regular and consistent recognition of achievements both in and out of the classroom. Positive feedback is given often and shared publically to highlight individual student achievement. It is communicated on posters, newsletters, and electronic announcements. Self-efficacy beliefs are advanced when peers help each other. Multiple opportunities are provided for this exchange.

Students have opportunities to stretch themselves to reach goals that originally seemed unattainable. For example, struggling students are paired with mentors who help and guide them in small steps to accomplish larger tasks. These opportunities are provided throughout the institution, both in and out of the classroom.

Take a look at the strategies in principle 3, "Promote realistic self-efficacy beliefs in each student," to see examples for integrating self-efficacy into the learning culture.

What Experiences Enhance Successful Learning?

An effective learning culture is only as good as its ability to continue and sustain successful learning. Learning must be contextualized to meet the needs of a diverse student body as well as faculty, staff, and institutional stakeholders. Is the student population primarily residential, commuter, or mixed? How many students are ready for the rigor of academic study? What barriers exist that may impede learning? What resources are available to address academic, financial, and emotional needs?

Sustaining successful learning involves asking relevant questions, honestly facing resource limitations, openly acknowledging resistance to change, exploring alternate pathways to supporting and advancing student learning, and taking a hard look at what we are doing.

We strongly encourage a systemic approach to developing a learning culture based on the Believe in You model. Involve all stakeholders and include students in planning, delivering, and evaluating all learning experiences both in and out of the classroom. Pay attention to efforts that promote persistence, emotional awareness, and self-efficacy in learning endeavors across all units.

Remember the potential of one person to encourage and enhance learning success, guide someone through difficult times, be the one who makes a difference, and believe in someone. In the words of Jonah, "I could talk to Dr. M. about anything ... She's always been there for me, always, from day one. From day one, she's always been there for me."

Ask Yourself

1. What concerns are creating a sense of urgency in my learning culture?
2. How will a guiding coalition be developed to address these concerns?
3. What do I want my learning culture to look like?

Appendix A

Instructional Strategies

WE HAVE ORGANIZED these sample strategies according to the five principles outlined in chapter 6. Although they are described individually, we encourage a holistic, integrated approach in the classroom. To be most effective, these instructional strategies cannot exist in isolated courses but should be integrated across the curriculum.

Principle 1: Facilitate a Growth Mind-Set

Rationale

When students understand the difference between a fixed and a growth mind-set, they can assess their own mind-set and develop strategies that are aligned with a growth mind-set. This mind-set correlates with increased motivation, learning, and achievement.

Learning Objectives

- The student will be able to distinguish between a growth and a fixed mind-set.

- The student will determine through a self-assessment which mind-set best describes his or her own tendencies.
- The student will learn at least three strategies for developing a growth mind-set.

Activities

- The facilitator will lead a discussion based on the conceptual framework below of growth and fixed mind-sets and how they may influence a student's motivation and ability to succeed.

Conceptual Framework

	Fixed Mind-Set	Growth Mind-Set
Self-belief	Capabilities inborn and not likely to change	Capabilities can grow through effort
Behavioral Tendency	Continuously tries to prove self to appear as capable as possible	Identifies strengths and weaknesses and continuously strives for improvement
Challenges	Avoid out of a fear of appearing deficient	Welcomed as opportunity to develop
Effort	Low-effort syndrome: Devalues effort, believing it proves lack of talent	Sees effort as necessary for growth and development

Response to Failure	Stops trying: Why waste time?	Considers it a challenge; interest in success increases; demonstrates resilience
Response to Criticism	Defensive, often attributing failure to others	Eager to utilize feedback to improve
Impact on Development	Avoids challenging situations, stays in safe environments	Thrives in challenging situations, often seeks them

Based on the work of Carol Dweck. Chart adapted from
http://solutionfocusedchange.blogspot.com.

- Students will independently complete a mind-set self-assessment and determine which mind-set best describes their tendencies. When they have responded to each of the four statements below, students discuss their results in small groups. Each group reports back to the whole with a summary of their discussion and examples from their personal experiences.

1. Your intelligence is something very basic about you that you can't change very much.
2. You can learn new things, but you can't really change how intelligent you are.
3. No matter how much intelligence you have, you can always change it quite a bit.
4. You can always substantially change how intelligent you are.

- Instructor will provide feedback for all course-based assignments based on the principles listed below for growth mind-set. Following major assignments, the instructor will lead a discussion around these principles. For example, when returning test scores, the discussion could be based on what strategies students might use next time to improve their grade. (This could be framed on internal locus of control rather than blaming the test or another external locus.) Students should be encouraged to compare their score on the current test to a prior test and think about what made the difference.
- Toward the end of the course, students will share the strategies they have learned to develop a growth mind-set and also the challenges they had to overcome and may still have.

Feedback to Promote Growth Mind-Set

Avoid	Include
Praising ability or intelligence	Praising and encouraging practice and persistence
Making judgments	Inspiring trust
Protecting from mistakes and challenges	Encouraging risk-taking
Highlighting mistakes	Learning from mistakes
Attributing success or failure to external locus of control	Attributing success or failure to internal locus of control

Principle 2: Create an Emotionally Supportive Environment

Rationale

When students are self-aware, able to manage themselves well, and socially conscious, they are better able to learn and succeed academically.

Learning Objectives

- Students will understand the concept of emotional intelligence (EI) and complete an emotional intelligence self-assessment.
- Students will demonstrate the use of their self-assessment results.
- Students will describe how they benefited from a service-learning experience.

Activities

- The facilitator will provide a reading assignment on emotional intelligence, and students will work in pairs to summarize it for oral discussion: "Emotional Intelligence Has 12 Elements: Which Do You Need to Work On?" by Daniel Goleman and Richard E. Boyatzis, *Harvard Business Review*, February 6, 2017.
- The facilitator will show a five-minute video on emotional intelligence and lead a discussion after the viewing: *Emotional Intelligence: An Introduction,*

https://www.youtube.com/watch?v=Y7m9eNo B3NU.

- Students will complete the following informal EI survey.

Emotional Intelligence Self-Assessment

Rate yourself on each capability:

1 = needs development
2 = adequately developed
3 = well developed

Self-Awareness

Capability	1	2	3
Emotional self-awareness: ability to read and understand your emotions as well as recognize their impact on work performance, relationships, and the like			
Accurate self-assessment: realistic evaluation of your strengths and limitations			
Self-confidence: strong and positive sense of self-worth			

Self-Management

Capability	1	2	3
Self-control: ability to keep disruptive emotions and impulses under control			
Trustworthiness: consistent display of honesty and integrity			
Conscientiousness: ability to manage yourself and your responsibilities			
Adaptability: skill at adjusting to changing situations and overcoming obstacles			
Achievement orientation: drive to meet internal standard of excellence			
Initiative: readiness to seize opportunities			

Social Awareness

Capability	1	2	3
Empathy: skill at sensing other people's emotions, understanding their perspective, and taking an active interest in their concerns			
Organizational awareness: ability to read the currents of organizational life, build decision networks, and navigate politics			
Service orientation: ability to recognize and meet the needs of others			

Social Skills

Capability	1	2	3
Visionary leadership: ability to take charge and inspire with a compelling vision			
Influence: ability to wield a range of persuasive tactics			
Developing others: propensity to bolster the abilities of others through feedback and guidance			
Communication: skill at listening and sending clear, convincing, and well-tuned messages			
Change catalyst: proficiency in initiating new ideas and leading people in a new direction			
Conflict management: ability to deescalate disagreements and orchestrate resolutions			
Building bonds: proficiency at cultivating and maintaining a web of relationships			
Teamwork and collaboration: competence at promoting cooperation and building teams			

Adapted from Goleman (1995).

- Students will meet in pairs and share survey results with each other.
- The facilitator will model how to develop a plan to strengthen one area of EI.
- Students will develop a plan to strengthen one area.
- The facilitator will provide a template for developing the plan.
- Students will share their plans with each other and offer suggestions as requested.

Template for EI Development

Area	Activity
Self-Awareness	
Self-Management	
Social Awareness	
Social Skills	

Principle 3: Promote Realistic Self-Efficacy Beliefs in Each Student

Rationale

Positive self-efficacy beliefs promote successful learning, while negative beliefs impede it. Realistic self-efficacy beliefs are most beneficial for successful learning results.

Learning Objectives

- Students will understand the concept of self-efficacy beliefs and how they affect learning.
- Students will complete a self-efficacy assessment and understand how the results contribute to their learning.
- Students will demonstrate how they overcame a low self-efficacy belief.

Activities

- Instructor will define self-efficacy and describe how positive, realistic beliefs contribute to successful learning. The instructor will share personal examples.
- Students will complete a subject-specific version of this informal self-efficacy assessment. Instructors will insert subject-specific tasks.

How sure are you of being able to do the following?	Not at all sure	Somewhat sure	Sure	Very sure

Adapted from Gibbons, Melinda M. (2005). *College-Going Beliefs of Prospective First-Generation College Students: Perceived Barriers, Social Supports, Self-Efficacy, and Outcome Expectations.* Directed by L. DiAnne Borders. The University of North Carolina at Greensboro. Retrieved from http://libres.uncg.edu/ir/uncg/f/umi-uncg-1049.pd.

- Students will meet individually with the instructor and share their self-efficacy survey results.
- Students will write a paper about how they overcame a low self-efficacy belief and replaced it with a realistic one. They will demonstrate the task they previously could not accomplish.
- Students will develop realistic goals for completion of specific course requirements. The instructor will individualize due dates for assignments based on the completion goals of each student.
- Instructors will use peers to demonstrate successful completion of a learning task.
- Students will be taught how to use metacognitive strategies, such as self-monitoring and self-testing, to improve their self-efficacy beliefs.
- Instructors will provide immediate feedback on learning tasks and emphasize the use of performance monitoring and evaluation.

Principle 4: Develop Student Grit through Alignment of Short- and Long-Term Goals

Rationale

Students will learn how to set realistic goals and understand the pathways needed to meet them. They will see through the flowcharts where measurable markers are along the way and also what alternatives exist when barriers are encountered.

Learning Objectives

- Students will articulate a long-term SMART goal.
- Students will complete a worksheet for their SMART goal.
- Students will develop a flowchart that creates pathways to their long-term goal with short-term options along the way.

Activities

- The instructor will lead a discussion on the components of a SMART goal based on the following conceptual framework that links goal setting to persistence.

Setting SMART Goals

Specific	• What do I want to accomplish long-term? • Why do I want to accomplish it? • What challenges do I expect?
Measurable	• How will I measure my progress? • What short-term goals are necessary to get me there? • What will I do if I encounter an obstacle?
Achievable	• How will I accomplish my long-term goal? • What steps do I need to take? • What options should I build in if I don't succeed with one short-term goal?
Relevant	• Is the timing right for me to work toward this goal? • What resources will I need?
Time-Bound	• How long will it take me to accomplish my goal? • What happens if I don't meet my deadline?

- Students will work in groups to answer the questions posed in the conceptual framework chart. They will be encouraged to challenge each other on their long-term goals and the short-term goals necessary to accomplish them. Through peer feedback, students will develop alternate pathways in case they meet obstacles along the way.

- Each student will develop a flowchart that clearly articulates the alignment of short-term goals with long-term goals. The flowchart must include options for new pathways if obstacles arise.
- Students will work in teams to help each other develop and refine their flowcharts using the symbols in the example below. These symbols will help the students see goal setting as a process with built-in markers along the way. Once the individual flowcharts are completed, the teams will present them to the whole group and provide a rationale for how the short-term goals align with the long-term goals.

Flowchart Example

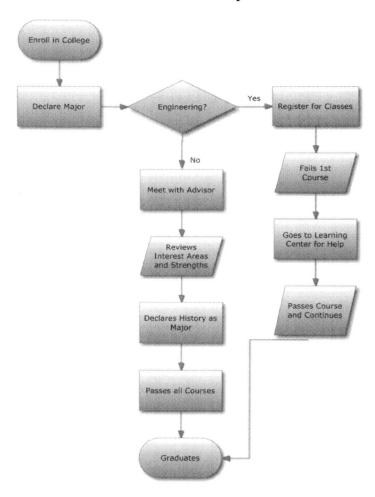

Principle 5: Strengthen Protective Factors to Increase Student Resilience

Rationale

Students will receive the support they need to see where their levels of understanding are compared to the expectations of the instructor for the content they are expected to master. The instructor will hold the class to rigorous standards while providing the scaffolding they need to succeed. Once they understand the gap, they can begin to work on study strategies to succeed at the appropriate level.

Learning Objectives

- Students will understand the six levels of Bloom's Taxonomy for the cognitive domain.
- Students will apply their responses to test items at the appropriate level in Bloom's Taxonomy.
- Students will understand the gap between their level of response and the correct response.
- Students will develop study strategies to narrow the gap.

Activities

The instructor will explain Bloom's six levels of cognitive understanding and provide specific examples from the course content related to each level of the taxonomy as described below.

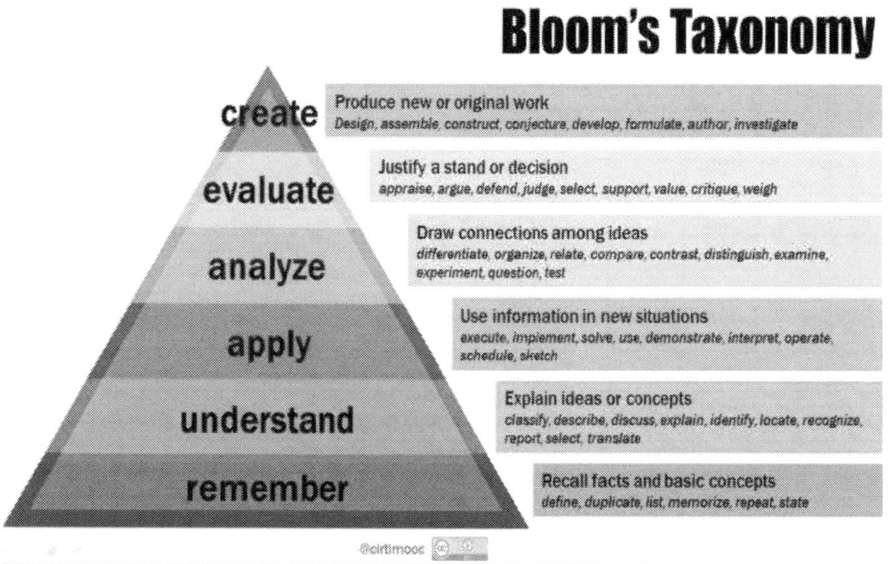

From Vanderbilt University Center for Teaching.

- The students will work in teams to label practice exam answers (provided by the instructor) according to Bloom's levels of understanding. Each team will present their results to the whole group with a rationale for their labels.
- Teams will develop exams that elicit different levels of understanding and give them to another team to answer. Each team will score the responses and label them with the appropriate level based on Bloom.
- Following several team-constructed practice exams, the instructor will begin giving exams designed to elicit different levels of understanding. In addition to answering the questions, students will label their own answers based on Bloom.
- Test feedback will include a discussion of the expected level of understanding versus the actual answers provided by the students.
- The class as a whole will discuss the different levels and study strategies for moving from one level to a more advanced level.

Appendix B

Interview Transcripts

The headings below were meant to provide a general framework for the interviews. The tone was more conversational and not linear or formal. Additional questions always occurred as student stories unfolded.

Questions

Demographics

- Please tell us your name and age.
- Tell us something about your family (e.g., number of siblings, educational level, your role at home).
- At what age did you start college?
- How many colleges have you attended? If you transferred, what caused you to transfer?
- Were you a full-time or part-time student?
- Did you work while attending college?
- What made you decide to attend college, and what were your expectations?
- Did you have specific educational goals? What were they?
- Did you expect to encounter barriers?

Student Story

Please tell us your personal story:

- What obstacles did you encounter and how did you overcome them?
- What helped you the most when you came up against an obstacle to your goals?
- What would you do differently?
- What advice would you give to other students? To faculty and staff?

Student Perspective

Please share your thoughts on the following statements:

- Your intelligence is something very basic about you that you can't change very much.
- You can learn new things, but you can't really change how intelligent you are.
- No matter how much intelligence you have, you can always change it quite a bit.
- You can always substantially change how intelligent you are.

The following transcripts were edited and organized into topics that emerged during the interviews to make them easier to read. They represent exactly the words of the students. We have permission from all students to share their stories, but we have changed their names to ensure their privacy.

Adam

Introduction/Background

Well, my name is Adam. I went to college in fall of 1999 at the age of eighteen. I'm unique from most students that I was diagnosed very early on in my life with a learning disability. I have dyslexia learning disability and it was very challenging for me to do well in a traditional school setting, so I had to take resource classes. I started off with special educational courses to ensure my success, and it was very challenging. Even though I had a good intellect, I had a hard time with writing and reading, and it was clearly evident on my SATs. And when I started college at Xavier, I was placed in remedial classes at Xavier because of my testing skills said I was a bit lower than most people. And because of that said, it started me up behind from most people.

And most people didn't think that I would actually be able to go to college with all this, with having a learning disability, taking remedial classes. People didn't think that this would be possible to overcome. Well, in order to understand how I overcame it, you got to understand my family background. I grew up in a very, very poor family with six brothers in a single mother household. My mother always stressed to us the value of education. She, herself, never graduated high school and my dad never graduated elementary, never finished past the fifth grade. But my mom always stressed that if you believe in yourself, put God first, and work really hard, you can achieve it. And one of the most strongest fundamentals is to have a strong family support, particularly a strong parent. That's one of the secrets, my biggest success secret was to have that parent support.

Faculty Interaction and Support

When I went to college, I started to form a group of people that I knew that would really care for me and I got to know the faculty. And when I was there at Xavier taking remedials I met one of the chemistry faculty member, Dr. Ann, and she said, "Okay, if you want to achieve it, I'm willing to work with you, but you have to be willing to put the work in too," and I said, "Yes."

And one of the things as faculty member that she did was that she went beyond what the normal call was, that most faculty members teach their class and leave. Well, Dr. Ann really cared for each one of her students and she knew the obstacle I had sat in front of me, so what she would do sometimes is that we would … first of all, she's like, okay, she helped me schedule my classes so where I had her for every single class for chemistry: I had her for chemistry lab, lecture, and drill. Therefore, I had the same consistent teacher so she knew as I progressed, you know, she knew what was covered, because she was the same teacher.

And that … working with that same solid teacher for all three classes really … first of all, it gave me confidence because I knew the teacher to work with; two, she got to know my learning style better, which I think is something that's very important for students who really want to do well, is try to get the same teacher to teach you as many classes in that particular subject as you can so you can develop a relationship. And her hard work and discipline in helping me ensured me that I was able to do it well.

Remedial Classes and Mainstream to Success

Um, a student from remedial ... when I took remedial classes, I would not take any class ... I was not allowed to take any real courses so ... I did well, but then ... right after I went into the mainstream working with Dr. Ann, working with a lot of the faculty members at Xavier, I was the first one in the school history for someone to take all remedials and then take eighteen hours the following semester and finish off with a 3.8. No one had ever done that at the school.

Being placed in the remedial courses really hurt me at first; you know my pride was hurt, because I wasn't expecting this, you know. I did pretty good in high school. I was thinking, you know, I could go in there, I had this thing, you know, everyone telling me I got scholarships ... you know, I just overcame all these other obstacles in high school to prove that I was worthy for it. So I didn't know I'd be there. And when I took it, it really made me devastated.

I felt like giving up. I wanted to quit. I thought that they made a mistake, that I didn't believe in myself, but my mom, you know, she cleans houses for a living and she worked hard to send her kids to college because she wanted her kids to go to college, and I called my mom. That's what made me really realize, you know, my mom believed in me, and the faculty believed in me, and I can do this, so I said "Okay." Even though I'm personally hurting, I know I can arrive above this. So that was the first thing that I had to focus in my mind-set, to say that, and learn that the remedial classes wasn't really a punishment, but it was really to enhance me because they want to make sure I can be successful and that was the first thing I had to change my positive ... my thinking around to be more positive.

And the second thing is that not being able to take the

classes, I felt kind of out left because all the other students are taking their classes. They're talking with each other about, "Oh, I did this equation," and you're sitting there, you know, basically going over algebra review. And you're like, you know, "I'm doing basic algebra, what are you talking about, chemistry and stuff?" And I felt very upset by it and frustrated, but I knew that I will get there if I keep on working with my ... if I keep believing in myself, and lo and behold, I was even helping people, even though I was taking remedials, people was coming to see me, if I knew anything about the chemistry, and I was amazed that I knew stuff that they ... they were taking the course and me in remedial, but I knew about it, and that showed me that I really can ... even though I'm not in that course, I know when I get there, I will be successful.

Getting Help

Really, it was the teacher believing in me and the teachers really taking the time. Really, it was a lady named Ms. Reed, and what helped me was that they took their time and analyzed what was the mistake and how they talked to me. They didn't say, "Well, oh, well, just do this." What they did was "Okay, you're having a hard time understanding and comprehending the difference between, um, opinion and facts," and Ms. Reed would get there at six in the morning, supposed to go to class at six in the morning, 6:00 a.m., and she like, "Okay, this is your problem," and she will work there, like literally go over one-on-one, and say, "Okay, this is what ... this is this, this is that," and have me explain to her what's she's teaching in my own words to her. And that one-on-one help really showed ... okay, this is the aha moment.

In mathematics, the teacher saw I was good so what he did, he'd have me come up to front of the board and teach the other students; therefore, it gave me more confidence too, because not only did I know it, but I was able to teach other students. So really, the one-on-one helped and then, you know, showing my strengths in the class and the teachers realizing my strength, and how well I can teach and helping others really helped me get through the remedial class, and also, just really having teachers who were really concerned. It wasn't just there for ... they really didn't treat the remedial classes as remedial classes; they treat them as college courses, and I guess it made you feel like, "Okay, you're in college." Even though it was remedial, you're in college and that really made the blow less devastating. It really, you know, helped you be like, "Wow, they really do believe in us!"

Goals and Encouragement

Yeah, when I first entered college, my goal ... my idea was that I wanted to go to finish undergraduate, go to medical school, and become a doctor. It's exactly what I wanted because I really liked the medicine and I really love science and mathematics. When I first got there, that's what my long-term goal was to be, become a doctor, but as time went on, I got into school, I did well, got exposed to research, and then I changed my academic goals to get a PhD, which I was very successfully to do ... I did in 2009. After I finished undergrad, I was able to go to graduate school and get a PhD.

When I first got to college and stuff, you know, some

people told me, you know, Xavier might not … the school I went to might not be the best school for me. And what the administrator, who didn't mean nothing by it, she just … the administrator was like, "Well, we don't know because it's a very science-oriented school and your skill set and what you have is lacking and it might not be the best for you; you might think about transferring to another school or either changing your major to something else that's non-science-related."

Sometimes, you know, just … I remember when I was recruiting for college and I went to one … I forgot the representative of what school it was … my mentor was with me and the guy was like … I'm like, "I'm interested in going to your school," and he looked at me like, "I don't think you really … I don't think you have the qualifications for it." And I told him about my SAT scores wasn't the greatest. He like, "No, I don't think you have the …" He didn't even want to talk to me, just brushed me off.

And also, because I grew up poor and in low-income housing, a lot of the people when they found out where I came from—I grew up in Southfield Village in Connecticut, in Stamford, Connecticut—people at first, when they don't know where I grew up from, they're like, "Oh yes, we're really interested in you! Yes!" I said, "Well, I grew up in a … you know, I grew up in low-income housing." People would just stop there in their tracks and be like, "Well, you know, you just don't quite fit what we're looking for."

My mom instilled us to really put God first, that's the first thing, my faith, and knowing that God has to come before me. Two was my mother's strong influence in us and raising her kids. She was like, you know, "Education is the key; you can do anything," you know. And my mother's dream … my mother dreamed that one day that her boys be able to wear college shirts and carry a briefcase to work—wear a shirt and tie and carry a briefcase to work. That's why I always wear a shirt and tie, even for this interview, because I'm living my mother's dream.

And the third thing was that I had the faculty when I went to Xavier and went to LSU who really believed and knew there was a challenge but instead of running from it, they worked with me even harder and they saw that I was going to put in … you know, most people only put in a mile worth of work … I was doing ten hundred miles and they saw that, you know, the late nights, the studying … and the faculty saw that and recognized that and they was willing to work there just with me.

And I remember Dr. Ann would start class at eight … at seven in the morning and, you know, most classes end at five, she was working with me alone until eight, nine o'clock at night 'cause she knew that I had potential of being a great student but it just took a while to get there, so those are the three things that did it. It was strong faith in God; strong support in family, particularly my mother; and great teachers who really went beyond just seeing the student. They went there and went, "Okay, you have the potential, it works a little bit harder, but you're worth the extra hours."

Advice to Students

Three things that I think of … the first advice is one: You have to believe in yourself and know, wherever you are, I don't care if you're a failing student; I don't care if you're an anxious student. You have to believe in yourself and know that you can do this. And particularly for students who are failing, they believe that they're in a downward spiral and they want to quit. You've gotta believe in yourself.

The second thing is, see yourself, see what you want to be. I always tell people, "Envision what you want to be. See yourself going across the graduation line, okay?" That's what your vision is going to be. Three: Make a plan. Make a realistic plan on, "Okay, how can I plan this?" Okay? Don't say that you want to graduate. Well, that's a big goal, but you need to think about do it for semester by semester by semester, month by month, week by week. Make a goal, okay?

Also, get to know your professors. Remember: you know it up here [points with the forefinger on each hand to each temple of his head], it might not come well on the paper sometimes, but sometimes the professors know [points again with the forefingers to his temples] that you know it up here and you speak to them, get that relationship going, "Oh, this person knows what they're talking about." And that happened to me sometimes, particularly in philosophy. I knew the material. I had a hard time writing, but I knew the material orally, so when I went to the guy, I was like, "Okay, listen, I know I didn't say it right in the paper, but this is what it is." And he's like, "You know, that's a great, great mind." He allowed me to redo the paper again. I didn't get off easy. He's like, "Well, redo the paper again, you know, I'll give you the credit because you told me that you mastered the material." Now, I redo the paper again to make sure I got a better grade. But I had a plan, and then I made sure I met my professor so they know who I was.

Those are things that I think a lot of students to fail to realize the importance of having a plan and gettin' to know the faculty member. And they said, "Well, why's it important to know the faculty member?"—because I can tell you about all the one-on-one, but I initiated a lot of it because I went to the faculty member and, you know, I said, "Listen, this is me. I have a learning disability. I'm a hard worker. I promise you I'll do the best I can." And they saw me on the first day, and they saw me sit in the front row, early on-time to class, being a model student, and that's when they went, "Okay, you want this bad enough. We're gonna go the extra mile for you." If your student is struggling and, you know, most of the kids get discouraged, you know, stop going to class, sit in the back, be disruptive … therefore, the teacher won't have that focus on you because you don't see that drive. But they see that drive in you. You can be a failing student, but if they see that drive in you, you really are serious; they're going to help you to make sure you succeed.

Advice to Faculty

The first thing I tell faculty and staff when I choose them is first of all, make sure you try to understand what you're trying to get to the students, and we are so trained and know our knowledge so well, that sometimes we forget how we're explaining it to students, and I always like to think about it this way: what if it were the first time I ever heard this; what can I use to help make sure I understand it? And that's the approach of keep it simple. I really say keep it simple. That's one of my best facts I tell them is keep it simple because you think that a lot of times that using these big words and using these concepts the kids are going to get it, but sometimes you have to break it down very simply. Particularly, I teach chemistry and you can be lost in a matter of seconds, but if you keep it simple and then slowly build them up, the kids will be okay with the approach.

Also, I'm a big proponent of having students teach and having them work in groups where students have to explain to each other or to you what they're doing because the problem is, a lot of times, you think the kids are getting it. Then they come to your office and be like, "Well, this is what I thought you was doing with the problem." I didn't really explain it that way, but this is how you interpreted it. But now if you catch that in the classroom, you know, just having group discussion real quickly, and be "Okay, now tell me what you guys think this, the answer is, and why?" Therefore, you can think about their pattern they're thinking in but, "Oh, this is what's going on, this is the problem."

I think that would be one of the major things. One, keep it simple, and two, try to get as much feedback as you can by having them explain things in their own words so you see whether or not they understand what we're teaching. And that's the best advice I'll give to most teachers starting off. And also, if you have the extra time, be willing to stay a few minutes after and get to know the students.

Intelligence and Success

You can change intelligence, it's just all how hard you're willing to work with it, you know. And why I tell you that: my life is the proof because you look at what I was faced with—a mother without an educational background, a father who didn't pass fifth grade—how would he have a son who is a PhD chemist? You know, and that tells you that, you know, if I did ... was supposed to have only what they gave me, I'm not supposed to be this far.

In summary, I'm a boy who grew up very poor in a low, single-income housing family. Neither one of my parents finished high school, and I had dyslexia. I was poor. I had all the obstacles in the world to give up. But with hard work and determination and the extra ... the teachers who sensing you never know when an impact ... when they'll have an impact on a student, I'm telling you that my professors in college, in high school, and elementary, because they really cared and saw that I had the potential, made a great impact, and to every teacher—*don't* [emphasis by speaker] give up on those students that just seem like they're not learning. You never know where your fruit of your labors is going to come in at. And for the students, I'm living proof: I got a PhD in chemistry. I don't say that to brag, but I say that so that we all can do anything that we achieve and believe in, and that's the message I want to make sure ... there's nothing that we cannot do if we believe in yourself and you're willing to work hard.

Calvin

Introduction/Background

I'm from Mansfield, Louisiana. I grew up with my mother and my father as well as my two older sisters, so I'm the only boy and the baby. I was blessed to be able to get a full scholarship to LSU in Baton Rouge. I went down there majoring in engineering, but that was not exactly working out for me. I was not the most attentive person in class [laugh] at that time. So then I transferred majors, trying to figure out what I wanted to do with my life. I always had the brain power to be able to do something, but I just never really honed in on one thing to do.

So I was fortunate to go to LSU, and I took my general

classes and everything ... actually, my grades got bad and I actually ended up flunking out of college after my father passed away from lung cancer. So once I got back, I met Dr. Saundra, and she introduced me to some strategies that helped me to realize my academic potential. I really questioned my abilities after I initially flunked out. However, she really restored my confidence, and she showed me the importance of just establishing a routine, going to class every day, and just getting something in my brain every day that has to do with my classes.

Adjusting to College

I made it there in '97, and I actually had two academic scholarships to LSU, but adjusting from a small town to a city was difficult. It's always ... it's easier to make the right decision when there's only two choices: you can study or you can play basketball, maybe play video games. But then when you get to a city where you've got your own friends; you've got email friends; you can go to the mall; you can go to the movies ... there's so many other things that can distract you from the task at hand.

Also, I was always the guy who made good grades, so I kind of took it for granted that I would do it. In middle school, people said that it would be difficult in high school, and then I got to high school and that was easy, and so people said it would be difficult in college, and I thought to myself, *Well, it hasn't been hard yet, so why would it be hard now?* And so then once things started getting hard, I kind of panicked and didn't act on the situation, not understanding the dire nature of the situation at hand. When you've never been ...

[Interruption from interviewer: "What was getting hard?"]

Um ... just the ... well, my grades just were not as good and, um, that was new to me. Everything that I've ever done in terms of my academic career, you know, going back from when I was a young boy, everything was easy, you know? I would take the tests and I would get a good grade. And I would take the tests, and I would get a good grade. And, you know, things always manifested itself to me, um, being successful in the classroom, and so when I wasn't, it just kind of freaked me out, to say the least. So that was the situation, and I didn't go ... I was too ashamed to go get the proper help that I needed at the time. I wanted to sort it out on my own.

Experiencing Failure

First, I started off around a 3.0. Then I lost my scholarship when I was around a 2.83, and that really took away some motivation because I needed a 2.85 and I thought to myself, *Two-hundredths of a point? I mean, really?* So then, I really, um, my grades really dropped, but one of the primary situations was I was not going to class. You know, when you don't have mom to get you up, you know, when it's all relying upon you, that's a very difficult situation. I was ... I was disciplined and naturally smart, so I didn't have to play by the quote/unquote rules in high school.

And then I got to college and, you know, I started slacking even more and that was a big, um, a big reason as to why my grades dropped off. You go to class on Monday and you don't get the stuff from, the information, from Wednesday and Friday, you know ... and I tell my students now … I equate it to this: if you have an instruction manual to build a table, and there are seven steps and you do step 2 and step 6 and you missed the rest of them, how will you build a table? You're missing those blocks of information, and that is what I was doing and did not understand, um, exactly what I was getting myself into and how difficult I was making my course to be.

Everything was so new to me, and it was just difficult to really sort out, and I kind of lost myself in a way. Well, I'll graduate because that's just what you do [chuckle]. Someone asked me that a while back about graduation while I was in college, and I said, "People graduate. That's just what you do," not getting the big picture, not being able to see it. I think it was at the end of '01 and going into 2002, um, where I was placed on academic probation.

Keeping a Secret

Well, the summer of '02 is when my father got cancer, and that's when the bottom fell out. Um, you know, I should have … I wanted to do better, but it was just hard because I was driving three and a half hours home every weekend trying to see him. Um, so I think that's the mess-up. I think I did a whole … I think I dropped … ended up dropping every class. I think it's a scholastic drop, I believe, where I didn't pass any classes, I don't believe. I might have passed one, um, and I was hiding it from my family. I was … 'cause my mom and my dad … oh, they [shakes head left and right, smiling] they would not have been happy. I was telling them that, you know, things weren't great but I'm doing okay, you know, I'm doing okay and it'll be all right.

But, I just didn't want to let them down, but I didn't

want to tell them, even though that would've been the best thing to do because they love me and they want me to do the best. So I wasn't telling them, but I couldn't tell anybody else either, 'cause I was too ashamed to go to anyone else that I did not know, you know? Had I gone to Dr. Saundra right then, it would have saved me a lot of headache.

February 2003 he passed away, and also the school found out I think that, um, I wasn't in school. It was the fall of '02 where I was kicked out, but I was still living on campus, so they found that out, and so that's when they gave me a couple of days just to get out. Um, so I ended up finding myself an apartment and, um … obviously, I'll have to work.

Journey Away From and Back to College

Now, I gotta make some money some type of way, no more financial aid. So I went to work at a call center making eight dollars an hour, which is not a lot of money, and I'm sitting there and I'm helping other people with math, and they're like, "Man, like, you're so great at math, you know, why're you not in school?" And people were like, "You're too smart to not be in college," and I'm thinking to myself, "Wow, I could be making more money if I were in an upper management position, but I don't have the degree that says that I'm smart, even though people know that I am, so since I don't have that evidence, that's a problem." And that's when it clicked to me how important college is.

A friend of mine, Ashley, helped me get a job coaching with him at a middle school. So I go there and I'm coaching the kids and the kids are responding well to me and they're doing great on the field and on the basketball court, and so the parents start asking about me because they could see the relationship I established with the kids. And … um … and so they're asking me, you know, "So, what are you doing with yourself?" and I was too ashamed to say that I flunked out, so I just told them, "Well, you know, I'm saving up money to get back in school after my father passed away." So they asked me what was my specialty, and so I told them mathematics. So then, um … one of the parents called me, and he said, "Well, what if I were to start paying you to tutor my kids?" I said, "Well, that would be great."

So I go tutor the kids and in one month they go from Cs to As in math, and so the word-of-mouth spreads and I end up kind of establishing a side business in tutoring. And so the same parent that started me in tutoring, he told me he was just watching me one day and I'm looking, and I'm looking intimidated because he has an intimidating type of presence, and I'm thinking to myself, "Oh, God, does he not like me or something?" But he was watching me, and he pulled me to the side one day and he just told me, "Okay, what happened, because you are too smart not to be in college. What happened?" And so I just told him the exact story I just told you, you know, and he knew somebody, and that person actually knew Dr. Saundra. I ended up meeting Dr. Saundra with the other guy, and so Dr. Saundra hears my story and she told me she was a little skeptical at first, but she made some calls and I ended up applying again and they ended up getting me back in. And this was in June of 2008, so I quit my job at the call center because I have to do well in school.

Gaining Confidence and a New Perspective

So I'm definitely questioning myself because I'm thinking to myself, "Well, maybe I was just high school smart, maybe I'm not as smart as I think I am, you know, I don't know." And so I get back in, and so I tell you some of Dr. Saundra's advice, some of her study habits and tips. But the most important thing besides tips that she gave me was confidence. She really made me believe that I was at a different place in my life and that I would be fine. She really helped to calm me down.

When she looked at my academic record, she just reinforced who I was. She reminded me of the things I had accomplished. She talked to me in a very calm manner, and she just gave me perspective on things, and she told me … she directed me as to some of the things that were going wrong. As far as me not going to class, she was saying no matter how smart you are, if you don't have the information, it does not matter. She taught me about previewing, you know, about previewing the material beforehand and being familiar with it so when you see it it's not your brain adjusting to something new and learning it, it's only just learning it. So she taught me about that.

She also taught me about reviewing my material and taking better notes, um, you know, using abbreviations and things of that nature, anything that would help me personally to remembering. Um, but she was big on me just studying for about forty-five minutes every night, she says, even if … even that small amount would just help me continuously retain information as opposed to having those gaps in my memory. I was blessed because my first semester back taking twelve … taking nine hours in the summer, I made a 4.0.

Goals and Achievement

So after that, I established my major as general studies because it would be the quickest way for me to be able to get out of school because I'm twenty-eight, going on twenty-nine at the time, um, and if I had gone back into mathematics, my quality point deficit was too great but I still had those fifty hours of math credit. So after that, you know, I had smooth sailing and those last forty hours that I was in school, I had a 3.4 GPA. First college graduate in my family.

Right now, I'm actually teaching math at a high school in Louisiana, and that time I was out of school helps me to be able to relate to the students 'cause I can walk in and say that "Hey, I had an $80,000 scholarship, and I lost it, but I still overcame that." So I think that helps me to really establish a rapport with my students because I can relate to the kids that are doing well and are used to making As 'cause I've been that guy, and I can relate to the kids that, you know, are struggling at studies because I've been that guy too.

Experiences with Faculty

I had two very different experiences with the professors while I was on campus. On the negative side, I had a professor that gave me a very bad grade on a paper and this was the second time I was in college, when I was, you know, handling my business. And I wanted to meet with him about that. First of all, he did not ... um ... he criticized my paper, and he talked about one thing that was not in there, and it was. And so he had to change my grade and upped it ten points on the spot. But this professor would not even shake my hand when I told him, I said, "Thank you for meeting with me," he said, "Oh no, that's not necessary." He talked about the fact that I was a general studies major, he said, "Oh yeah, that figures." And then when I'm getting ready to leave the office, he says, "Oh yeah, good luck with your general studies degree." Now, I was, you know, say I'm twenty-nine years old at the time so I'm more mature, so I just kind of brushed over it even though I still obviously didn't like it, but I can't imagine if I were eighteen or nineteen, how I would have reacted in that situation.

So that was a very negative experience. Now in the positive experience, I'll never forget this lady—Anna. She was actually getting her PhD. Best professor I have ever had. She was so passionate, entertaining, but you could tell she really loved what she was doing, and I really learned in her class. I really did. And, uh, she … she's actually my model for being a teacher because she covered everything and, you know, she was friendly, but if you didn't care, you know, she didn't put up with any stuff either, you know. And if you showed you didn't care then you're on your own, but if you showed you cared, she would go to the ends of the earth for you.

Advice to Students

For the students, one thing, and this was Dr. Saundra's suggestion, was to go to the professors early in the semester the first day of class, and let them know, you know, that you expect to do well in their class and you look forward to their class. That way, a teacher can put a name and a face to you, and they're already seeing you in a positive light because a lot of professors, you know, if you're sittin' in the back and everything, they're going to have a certain perception of you because no matter what, even though professors are supposed to be a certain way, they're human, too, so you have to appeal to their human side.

So, you know, greet yourself to the professors; go see them on their office hours. Don't be lazy. Sit in the front of the class, preferably toward the middle, but definitely in the front of the class, so you can make that eye contact because there's something about having a vibe with a person that may gravitate them toward you or vice versa. So you may pick up on little things just from being closer in the class.

Another thing is just to go to class every day and do some form of studying every day. And the thing is, even with Dr. Saundra's suggestion, I didn't really study that hard. I just took the time to open the book and just skim over some things. Just rereading my notes gave me greater understanding because it's one thing to have an understanding when a professor is going over it, but professors go so fast, your main priority right then is to get the information down. If part of your brain is focused on getting the information down, then let's say if you're using 30 percent of your brain to get the information down, you only have 70 percent to learn it. But once you have it down, you have 100 percent of your brain just to learn it, just to focus on the learning aspect of it. So that would be another suggestion.

Buddy-up with someone, with the other people in your class, just in case you do end up missing a day. Get someone that you trust or someone you think you can trust, anyway, so that you can get the notes from them. Don't cram. Oh man, those overnight … it does you no good. It does you no good, doing all-night cramming. And, um, the way I look at it now is that if you know your stuff all the way, once the test comes, it's just like a review, as opposed to trying to learn at the end.

Intelligence and Success

Intelligence, to me, is your ability to focus on learning the task at hand. Many people have that ability, but some people choose not to use it. They choose to focus on other things. For instance, you may have a student who is really good at math; might have another one that's good in English. And that just may be the nature of people. However, you have some students that are not doing well in class, but they know the name of every song out there. They're intelligent in that realm, but they are putting their focus and intelligence in that realm as opposed to putting it into the realm of their academics.

So I disagree that intelligence is fixed. It is not fixed. And also it could just be the way that someone presents the material to you. Different presenters sometimes give you different results. You know, as intelligent as I came out to be in high school, I did not make it through college the first time. But even though I failed out, I regained myself and, you know, made it happen.

Jude

Introduction and Background

Okay. My name is Jude. I'm thirty-five years old. I have one brother. I have no parents and all my other grandparents are deceased as well. So it's just pretty much me and my brother. Um … he is a year older than me. He'll be thirty-six.

113

Well, my father was murdered when I was a baby, and my mother gave me up, so my grandparents are the ones that raised me and then they ended up becoming deceased as well, throughout my journey. And ... other than that, it's just been me. I am currently a full-time student at Ivy Tech Community College here in Bloomington.

High School

Well, during high school, I ran cross-country. I was on the swim team. I played in band. Made somewhat good grades, but then I just fell into the wrong people and ended up dropping out, and really wasn't too concerned about my education until I got older, and then I was looking at all these people getting this education and ... you can't even find a job at McDonald's without having to have a degree. So I just went ahead and put my foot down and got my GED and figured out what it is that I wanted to do and decided to become a student here at a college.

[Clarification from interviewer: "Got in with the 'wrong people.'"]

Um ... those were the type of people that cared more about themselves than anybody else. They'd say, "Hey, let's skip school" or "Let's go do this" or "Let's not do that but let's go over here and drink" or "Let's go over here to this party." Those were the kind of people that influenced me in dropping out of college ... or, I mean, high school.

Financial Challenges

Well, I was struggling financially, and then I just got tired of struggling financially and decided to get a job; every application that I got or anywhere that I tried to apply for, you needed an education. And most GEDs are required to work anywheres these days. So in order to better myself and make more money in order to be productive, I had to get the education.

Um ... I got my GED in about ... it took me two months to get my GED. But I studied every day and I studied for three hours a day, sometimes maybe four, and I just put my work down. And then I had resources like tutors that would help me if I had any questions. So, I mean, there was positive people that influenced me a little bit.

Significant People Who Helped

Um ... they were ... they were at the ready. You can find them online, but I went to the local library and actually they had, um, classes there for GED and then I just got in touch with them instructors and said, "Hey, I've been doing this on my own. I'm having a little trouble in this area right here. Would it be possible for me to talk to you?" And they didn't have one problem with it.

Starting College

Well, then I got a decent job, but I'm an artist and I love to draw portraits and things like that, so I wanted to get into that type of field, so I decided to enroll in a college. And this is my first semester in college and I had no idea what I was getting in for whenever I wanted to become a student at a college, even community college. And I was just determined that I am going to succeed no matter what and, like you said, resources are a big part, even here at the college. You would not believe how the impact of your professors or your tutoring centers or even the library clerks here that will help you.

Surprises

Oh, the amount of work that I had to do! That was a big surprise. But, I tell you, the English composition was probably one of the most difficult subjects because it is so demanding and you've got to write and rewrite and edit and revise and then rewrite it again. And after you get that determination and once you figure it out and how the formats go, it's just like a formula for math and then it just seems to fall into place. It just takes a little time, that's all.

Coursework and Studying

I got two English classes, as a matter of fact, on this semester right here, and then I'm taking Life and Object Drawing 1, and then Student Success for Ivy Tech. The Student Success course is how to manage your time; read and annotate articles properly; how to be a productive student as far as management goes.

Um ... it's helped me a lot because it allowed me to effectively utilize my time instead of spending so much time on one area and focusing on one aspect of my degree. I needed to focus on the whole aspect. So I broke it down, made up schedules like I done seen in the book and worked a couple of hours on this project, a couple hours on that project, a couple hours on this project, and then, most importantly, you've got to have time for yourself, and some things like that. So, it helped me a lot. I study every day, probably about four hours each day.

Employment

Yes. I am a full-time employee. I put in fifty-four to fifty-six hours a week. I am a ... I'm a cook at a restaurant, at Route 67 in Worthington. Yeah, I not only cook but I'm also the manager. I place all the orders, and I open and close every day.

Um ... now I go to college two days a week which is Tuesdays and Thursdays, but in the morning time I don't have to be at work until nine so I'm up by six in the morning doing homework and then I come home at ten at night and I put in another hour or so.

I'm always tired, but it's for the greater good.

Goals

Um ... well, I'm planning on getting my degree in visual communications, which is like a 3-D computer graphic and design. That's my passion; that's what I love to do, and they always say if you can do what you love then you won't work a day in your life. So that's what I'm trying to go for! But the Ivy Tech Community College doesn't offer the degree in the visual communications, so I have to earn a certain amount of college credits and then maintain my GPA in order to transfer to a facility that does.

Tough Times

Well, to get through the tough times, I believe that it created a sense of maturity. You know, I couldn't go and do this and I couldn't go and do that because no one else was going to do these other things that I had to do for me. So I had to just buckle down and learn responsibility, and that's what helped me a lot. And in my artwork ... well, it acted as a type of therapy to lead me through as well. Um, it allows me to express myself emotionally.

Even though I don't have to say words or I don't have to do anything, I can just sit in a room and I can listen to music and just get lost in my artwork and I don't have a care in the world. Um ... if I draw a picture, it would look like a black-and-white photograph. I specialize in photorealism.

Faculty Support

Oh ... my professors! They are amazing people, and they are highly helpful here, and if it wasn't for them I probably wouldn't succeed like I do.

Um ... well, like my professor in English 111. Her name is Ms. Christine. She will point out each individual's obstacles and then she will provide you with material or she will do anything that she can in her power to help each individual person. Because each individual person in these classes have different barriers and she has the ability to recognize them barriers and provide you with the right information and the right tools to overcome it. She is an amazing person.

Well, my organizational skills are good, but whenever it comes to me writing papers, sentence-level stuff, it's what

I have a little trouble with. So she took it upon herself to go out of her way to get me a book on grammar that would take me back of what I may have missed in high school and to reiterate that to where I can apply it to my college-level skills.

Well ... I've got ... my Professor Ingrid, she is my art teacher. And she is ... she is also amazing. She has supported me, and she will just come over to you, whenever I'm doing my artwork or something, and if she sees something ... she's just got a whole different perspective whenever it comes to art as what I do. And she can always ... she can always provide me with information that helps you. Even if you are stuck on an area, she knows what to say to help you overcome, to give you that emotional support.

Advice to Students

I would tell them to communicate. Communication in a college is the most important aspect that a student will need here. It is a valuable tool. If you don't communicate with these people and become friends with them, then they won't make you feel wanted, and then it'll make it hard for you here.

Um ... me, personally, I communicate with everybody. Whether it be the lady behind the desk or my professors or the student sitting beside me. I try to participate in the college ... what are they called ... um ... activities, so to speak. And I just try to be an active part of the community. There's a lot of good people here, and most people here have your best interests at heart and you shouldn't feel shy.

Advice to Faculty

Well, from what I have seen so far, they have done an excellent job with me. Whenever I come in and I know that what they're doing is successful, and I wish them to carry on that. Don't be afraid to reach out and talk to these students or providing them with information. Even though my professor provided me with a book to help me with my grammar, she didn't know if that would offend me or not. But I'm glad that she did because that didn't offend me.

Challenges Ahead

Well, time management because I will be taking four classes next semester as well, and I know I have Introduction to Microsoft Computers. I got English 202. I got Art History, so it's going to be ... I know that I got my time set for this and it's going to be an obstacle but as far as academically being prepared, I think that my experience in this first semester has boosted my confidence level enough to where I think that I can conquer the next one.

Reflections

Well, my brother ... his name is John. Like I said, he's a year older than me and he was one of them persons who was highly intelligent. He's got ... I don't know ... he's got, like, three degrees and then he got ... he graduated from two different colleges at the same time. They ended up giving him a degree of excellency. But whenever it comes to average, just everyday life, he just don't have a lick of common sense. He don't get it. He's always in and out of trouble, and I just hate to see it go to waste like that. I hate to say it, but he's incarcerated.

Well, he influenced me a lot, believe it or not, because here I sit, and I see a man that's got three college degrees and he's got a degree of achievement and when he did have a job he was washing dishes at a restaurant. And then I'm thinking, why would you apply the time and do all that work for them degrees and do something that doesn't even apply to it? It just makes no sense, so I don't want to end up like that. I'm going to make sure that I'm going after what it is that I'm going to apply myself to. So he did help me see that.

No. I don't see him and I don't ... if somebody's not beneficial to me or where I'm headed, then I try to distance myself from people who try to drag me down. Does that make sense?

No matter how much you love somebody, if they're not beneficial to your success, then they shouldn't be a part of you.

Intelligence and Success

Um ... I do believe that you can always substantially change your intelligence. I believe that. No one ... if anybody believes that they can't change the way they think about something or educate themselves, then they're wrong because anything ... you can learn anything that there is. The mind is a very powerful thing, and I do believe you can retain knowledge at any age, at any stage, as long as you have the will and the power to do it yourself.

Message to Students

For any student that's out there that has the ability to want to further their education and you're entering a college, do not be afraid to ask for help and utilize every resource that you have available to you, because that's what they are there for. The tutoring centers are amazing people, your professors are the *best* probably possible best resource that you can have because they are very knowledgeable about what they are teaching, and do not be afraid to ask. Nobody is ever ... the smartest and most intelligent people in this world didn't get where they are because they already knew what they know. They had to ask somebody, and they had to start exactly where we are, and I guarantee they had to ask too.

Jonah

Introduction

My name is Jonah. I'm twenty-five years old. My family? I have a younger sister; she's nine years old. Her name is Jillian Love ... my mother, Merty, and my stepfather, Elvis. I moved to Tennessee when I was about six years old from Evansville, Indiana, and this is my home. I love it. I'm glad we moved down here. I really enjoy it.

I started college at the age of twenty-two. This is my first time attending State Community College. I've never attended any other colleges besides State. I am what you would call a three-fourths-time student. I take anywhere from nine to eleven credit hours because of my work schedule. I work two jobs. I work at Fred's Discount Store, and I also work at the school as a mentor tutor.

I went to high school at … [laughs lightly and smiles] … my freshman year, I attended a Christian private school, my freshman and sophomore year. My junior year I attended Madison Academic, and my senior year I graduated from high school.

Struggles and Challenges

Between eighteen and twenty-two, I went to jail. I … I was facing two felonies. A guy had called me one day, wanted to rob my job, and because I did not call the police, I received twelve years for it. So I served two years in jail with ten years' probation. When I was released at the age of nineteen, I went to work in a factory to pay off all my fines and court costs. After working in a factory for about two and a half years, I was laid off, and I lost everything. I lost my house I was staying in, my car, all my furniture; everything got tooken from me. So … so then I went to Ripley, Tennessee, to live with a relative. I had a cousin who was sick (he's on dialysis), and I went down there to kind of watch out for him and kind of clean up for him and, I guess, in return, he let me stay with him. So while I was staying in Ripley, I just made up my mind. I was sick and tired of being … I feel like I was missing something, and that was my education.

Starting Over

I just got fed up with the life I was living. I decided to … the best way to make it through these ten years on probation was college. And that's when I decided to buckle down and come back home to Jackson and register for State.

After coming back home, back to Jackson, I went to

school and everything started to click for me. I got involved with my teachers. I told them about my story. I see it as a testimony because I took something negative and turned it into a positive. This is my fuel. I think about where I could have been five years ago and where I'm at now, to keep me to have that determination, that perseverance, to keep going forth in my education. I became good friends with Dr. M. She was my developmental teacher and she really helped me to open up and to speak up in class. You know, if I have a question, don't be afraid to ask.

Reflections and Regrets

With … with my probation, it … it was … it was hard. It was hard because I think about the scholarships that I lost. I was a basketball player in high school. All throughout high school I played sports. Basketball was my passion, and by me losing one of my scholarships to Missouri Baptist Community College, it hurt. It hurt me tremendous. Also, I lost a scholarship to … University of Memphis had offered me a scholarship, a full-ride for the ROTC program for the air force. My senior year I got involved in the ROTC program, and there I was the first corps commander of my senior year, and that really taught me the self-discipline. So I had all these traits, you know, and expectations of going to college, and I faced an obstacle, and that obstacle was the felonies. And it hurt me, it hurt my family, my teachers, my instructors, my dad … it's like I let everybody down.

Expectations and Getting Help

At first, I was expecting this to be a getaway. This was a time for me to not look at my past but look toward the future. I was expecting when I go to college to … to not look at the negative. I wanted to … to just concentrate on the positive because [slight chuckle, big smile] it seemed like growing up, it was nothing but negatives in my life. College really helped me out; it helped me focus, and it kept me out of trouble.

What helped me do that was … was the homework, the encouragement with the teachers. Oh my God! My teachers … they come to me [slight chuckle, big smile] and they always got encouraging things to say, and they … they really … they told me, "We see a lot in you, Jonah. A lot of potential is in you." And for me to share my story with my peers in my classroom, that … that really … because if I can give … if I can let them know anything about the streets and especially making the right decisions, you know, what goes on outside, don't let that change who you are. You can be anything that you want to be. You can … you can be a scientist. My major is chemistry. So I look at science as my getaway and that's really, really helped me.

Facing a Setback

Just recently, I had violated my probation, and I was in jail for four weeks, and upon my court hearing—I didn't know anything about this—but about six of my professors showed up to court and they spoke on my behalf. And the things they had to say was … it brought me to tears. I was a role model. I was a positive influence in the lives of my fellow students. And the result of that was the DA tried to give me ten years, make me serve my ten-year sentence in prison, but the judge said, "Mr. Irvin, you have pleased the courtroom." He said, "By your GPA and your hard work in school, we're going to let you … we're going to set you free."

My professors, they spoke on how … how I … [clears throat] for one instance, Mr. B., my trigonometry and calculus teacher, he said that "I didn't think Mr. Irvin was going to make it out of trig, trigonometry," and [chuckle, big smile] he said, "Man, he got in there; he buckled down; and he passed my class with an A." And that … he said, "He has a determination about himself." And hearing those good things just added more fuel to my fire inside to want to do well in school, to want to not please everybody but please myself. I want to make it not only in life, but also in school.

Factors of Success

My time management … with work and school, I had to find the time to really just focus on trigonometry, so I dedicated two hours a day. Two hours every day of the week to trigonometry and all of my other courses as well. And that really … that really helped me out a lot. I did.

I went to our writing center [big smile, shakes head]. Starting out, I was a terrible writer, terrible writer. My grammar, punctuation, I didn't have no style. So I went to the writing center and before every paper just to revise. I had trouble coming up with thesis statements. So I went there and they sit down and they worked with me for about two hours, and then I'd leave and go to work. And I would do that before I turned in every paper. And I took the … what they were saying, and I applied it. I just … I'd lock it in my head, and I applied it to every paper that I wrote. And it turned out I … I had some pretty tough Comp teachers [slight chuckle, big smile]. One teacher, he had gave me a D in Comp 1, and I was not happy with that grade. I said, "I know I can do better; I need to spend more time with writing." So I retook Comp, and I passed with a B+. And I was pleased with myself. My … my teachers, they … the writing center we had, they stopped me. They said, "Look, break down each paragraph." So I broke it down, and I just took it one paragraph at a time. And it has really worked out; and it's helped me in the long run.

I'm an open person. I love to speak and to greet everybody and to talk to them, not only in the classroom but outside the classroom. And they always greet me with a smile [this all said as he is smiling grandly]. And I see that as an opportunity to get in there and to talk with them. And that … I love State. That … it's like home. It's a small college, but it's a lot of love in the college. The teachers, they really care about the students. They really do.

Where I grew up at was a lot of gangs, drugs, and I … I didn't get involved in that. Once I moved to where I'm at now, I stayed to myself. I'm pretty much a loner. If I'm not at work, I'm at home or at school. The community? I wouldn't know too much about it. I wouldn't. I left that alone years ago.

What I try to do, at least, is to talk to the younger youth through my community service work that I do. I tell them about my story, how I've overcome, and how I'm in college now pursuing my dreams and my major in chemistry and just praying to God that they will listen and take heed with what I have to say.

Advice to Students

Don't give up. Don't give up. No matter how hard life may seem, do not give up. You can always change. You can change who you are. You can change your whole mind-set because I know: I have done it. And if ... set yourself away from the negative people that are around you, the negative influences. State has done that for me. It's nothing but positive influence in college. And I would recommend *anybody* [emphasis by speaker] to go to State. I tell them, I said, "Don't be ashamed because it's a junior college; sometimes you have to crawl before you walk." You have to. And I tell them to just focus in and don't give up when life throws you lemons. Make lemonade.

Toward the Future with Mentors

My educational goal is to receive a master's in chemistry. I want a master's in chemistry. Yes ma'am, I'm pursuing it. I went over it in my head many of times that I'm going to stay in college until I come off probation and I come off it in 2017. So I have plenty of time to reach any type of educational goal that I have set for myself. I look forward to ... I love to learn. I love to learn. That's one of my passions [chuckle, big smile]. I was sitting here thinking about my ... one of my favorite TV shows ... the History Channel ... and I just love to take in, to learn, and to apply it to life.

I acquired it from growing up: my mom, my mom. I remember as a young boy, my mom had a chalkboard in the kitchen, and she would sit down with me to work with my ABCs and my numbers. My mom, she's an evangelist, so growing up we would study the Bible about three hours every day. We'd have Bible study. And to have that knowledge of the Bible and be able to quote Bible scriptures ... we also had a nursing home ministry. So I would go and teach lessons with the elderly. And I enjoyed it. I really did. And I used that in college. I applied that same method to college. Whatever I learned, I tried to share it.

Academically, I see ... it's ... there's a lot of obstacles. I know that, as I reach my ... the upper levels in chemistry, in math, that's going to take a lot of ... a lot of time to get my studies in and to get a foundation set for myself; it's the time management, finding the time to do all this and work at the same time and do community service. It's a lot on my, my plate is full [chuckle, big smile]. I have a full plate, but I just pray to God that he keeps me focused, that I might be able to receive my goals.

I was kind of ashamed because of my age. I figured that this would be a course for a lot of students coming straight out of high school, but I had to remember that it's been years before I was in high school. I think I was out of school for about four years, and I forgot everything that I had learned [laugh, smile]. Everything! And when I went to class, I saw a lot of students my age in class. I also ... Dr. M. ... she helped me with ... she gave me extra books of writing: writing handbooks, different types of mechanics, all kind of worksheets that I could take home and use for myself. And her advice was "Mr. Irvin, you can do it." She called me Mr. Sunshine.

I thank God for Dr. M. That's, like, one of my ... my mentor, my role model. I look up to her a lot. I just finished taking her speech class. She also teaches speech at State, and I love the way that she's able to overcome her nervousness before each class and how she's ... she's active. She's always moving. I look at that, and I add it to my repertoire and my style of speaking. And Dr. M., she's a terrific person. I love Dr. M.

I go to Dr. M. I also talk to Minister Ray. He's a janitor at State, and I go to church with him when I don't have to work, and I talk to him about a lot of personal things. Dr. M., I talk to her about a lot of personal things. Mr. Britt [chuckle, smile]. Ms. White. Just about all of my professors, I talk to.

The word "mentor" means to me is a person that you can look up to. I admire Dr. M. A lot of traits we share the same. We have the same amount of energy in the classroom. We have a very, very bright personality. I could talk to Dr. M. about anything. She ... she always has good advice. She's never told me anything wrong. She's always been there for me, always, from day one. From day one, she's always been there for me.

Intelligence

You can always change ... you can always add. This statement here it's ... Wow! I don't see it as basic. Basic is something that is average. You know, this is something that's going to get you through. This is something that, your intelligence, is going to get you that job. It's going to put food on the table. That's what helps you be a provider, what you know, and I don't see it as very basic. And you can change. You can change very much, you can. I do believe that. It's like a, it's like a plant; it's like a plant. And as long as you're feeding it, it's going to grow. It's going to grow.

Kristen

Introduction and Background

My name is Kristen and I'm twenty two. So I actually grew up living with my grandma. She is, I think, sixty-five. She has two bachelor's degrees, one in, I believe, social science and then one in software engineering. She worked for Lockheed Martin Space Systems for twenty-five years. She retired just a few years ago. My mom is thirty-eight. She doesn't have any college degree or anything like that. She worked for Lowe's. I have a little sister who is graduating high school this year, and she has a one-year-old son.

Well … so, as you might have noticed, my mom is really young. She's only thirty-eight. And, so, when she had me, she just wasn't ready, so I lived on and off with her for … between her and my grandmother until I was fourteen and then I moved with my mom from California to Texas and then I lived with her there for eight months and then … um … everyone in the family decided it would be better if I lived with my grandma, so I moved back to California to live with my grandma. And then I lived with my grandma there for a year and then me and my grandma moved here, to Butte, Montana, and I've lived here since.

Um, well, she [sister] actually lived with my mom up until August of this year so I didn't really talk to her much until this year so I hadn't talked to her a lot, a lot, until … for nine years really. So, uh, it's good now though. I just moved out of my grandma's house at the beginning of this month and, uh, she still comes up—my sister—comes up and visits me at my apartment and, you know, we have a good relationship as far as sisters, you know, are concerned.

Um … I met my dad once when I was fourteen but that's it so no, not really a relationship.

Early School Years

Um … honestly, I was always really ahead of the curve, but it … I got bored really easily … um … so I would talk a lot, get into a lot of trouble, and that's kind of how it always was, all the way up through high school, up to … kind of up to the point where I stopped doing what I needed to do because I just didn't care enough anymore. Um, then in high school, I skipped school a lot. I got to the point where I almost didn't graduate, but I was really into sports. I played soccer, and so my soccer coach got me into track so that I could keep my grades up enough to play soccer in the fall. And so I ended up doing obviously well enough to graduate.

Um … not with police, really, just trouble, like, with skipping school and, you know, talking back to the teachers and, you know, all the teenage stuff that you look back on and you're like, "God, why didn't she just stay quiet?" Those kinds of things. You look at the kids now and you're like, "Oh, God, I was never like that!" But I was totally like that.

Starting College

So, my grandma, she was … you know, I told you she worked for Lockheed Martin and she was a software engineer … so she was … she really pressured me to go to college, which I'm glad she did now, looking back. So I basically had no option. If I wanted to have a place to live, I had to go to college. And so I applied to Tech—Montana Tech—and I went there and I basically didn't go and I failed out and they put me on probation and … um … so I was like, "Oh, God! I can't fail out of college. My grandma will never, you know, forgive me."

And so, I was like, "Okay, this is all that I needed. I can go back. I can do this." And so I went back, but I basically did the same thing. I kind of … I went for a little while and, you know, I went to classes for a little while and then I did the same thing. I stopped going, and I failed again. I failed. So the first semester, I failed all four of the classes I was taking. Um … and then the second semester, when I went back, when I was on probation, I failed two of the four classes I was taking. So I ended up getting suspended.

I think I just wasn't prepared. I think I just wasn't ready for college. I think I just … I don't even know that I knew what I wanted to do. I was going into liberal studies. Um … you know, I just … I was going for somebody that wasn't me. I was going to please my grandma and not because I was ready to go, and so I think that was the biggest thing for me was that it wasn't for me, which I think is what college is supposed to be about. It's an engineering school really, so it's really rigorous. Montana has an open university system, so everybody gets in, basically, it's what it is. I mean, our acceptance rate is really high. I think it's like 80 or 90 percent, but our courses are extremely rigorous, so they're really hard to get through. And so if you're not prepared for them, I mean, they're so tough.

So, basically, when you're suspended, you have to take a semester off, and so I worked at the gas station, and that's when I realized … I was like, "Oh my God! I cannot do this for the rest of my life. I have to go to college, like, I need a college degree. I can't be a manual laborer, minimum wage worker for the rest of my life. This is not me." Because even though I wasn't ready at the time, I always knew my whole life that I was going to go to college. You know, growing up with my grandma, I knew that I wanted to be successful. I think just at the time I wasn't prepared, you know? Um, and so I kind of just spent a semester working and realizing that I was ready to go back to college now.

Starting Over

So, um, I reapplied, because that's what you have to do after you get suspended. You have to reapply, fill out a new application, things like that, and so I did all of that new freshman stuff again, you know, buy all your books, pay your tuition, all of that stuff, signed up for my classes. Except this time, I went into computer science, which is basically what my grandma did. And I actually, I really liked it. I got close with my adviser and, um, I did well in all my classes. I got really good grades except that I realized I was a terrible programmer. I absolutely suck at computer programming. But I'm really good at math, is what I realized.

And I think I always knew that growing up, that I was really good at math except I don't think I realized it when I was in college until I realized I sucked at programming. It's that, I was still really good at the math behind the programming, and the computer science department and the math department at Montana Tech are in the same building, and so what I did is, I talked to one of the math professors, and she got me into the math department. And, so, I actually switched over to the math department, and that's where I've been ever since. And I actually joined the statistics department as well.

So in order to replace them [grades], you have to retake them, and they're still on my transcripts, so my ... when you look at my academic transcripts, my first two semesters still have them but they have letters next to them so ... I can't remember in which order they go, but they are Is and Es, and I actually have no idea what they stand for, but once you've retaken them, there's one letter next to them and when you've retaken it, the new one that you've retaken it with has a new letter next to it, and so they're both on there now, the one that has the F and the new one that I retook with the new grade. And so ... and then they replace it in my GPA so I still have the F on my transcript but in my GPA it's replaced with the A or the B or whatever I got ... So I literally went from a 0.0 my first semester to ... um ... my GPA recalculated as it's recalculated before this semester, I had a 3.51.

Factors in Success

I got really lucky with my first adviser. He ... so our ratio of women to men, or men to women, is seven to three at Montana Tech, so when I joined the computer science department, my adviser was absolutely ecstatic. He did everything he could to make it a really good experience for me. He wanted so badly for me to stay in the department, and so he had me work on projects with him, and he got me into all the classes that he could that he thought would be fun. And so he tried really hard to make it a good experience for me.

I felt really bad switching out of the department because of how hard he worked. I just ... I wasn't a good programmer, and I didn't enjoy programming like I knew that I should. But, yeah, he was definitely the first one at Tech to make me want to be there and make me enjoy college.

And then once I got into the math department, I decided that I wanted to tutor because I wanted to help people love math as much as I did, and so that was the next thing I did. I became a supplemental instruction leader, and so that was the next thing I did. I became an SI leader. And so, basically what that is, it's a TA who doesn't grade and what you do is you go to class with them, and you take all their notes and things with them, and then three times a week, you host one-hour tutoring sessions specifically for that class.

Um ... and I've been doing that since I came back to school, and I actually was the head SI leader last semester, but I ... like this past one ... I decided I didn't want to do that for this coming semester, just because it's been really overwhelming, but ... yeah ... so that was a really good experience for me. My adviser for that, she's been fantastic. She ... actually, I've been doing undergraduate research with her. For the last two summers, I've been her research assistant. So she has been one of the most fantastic faculty to work with because she's given me not only the opportunity to be an SI leader, but also to do undergrad research, which has given me the opportunity to present at conferences and to travel and to do things like that, so she's been really great!

Reflections on College Experience

Honestly, I think it worked out well for me. I think the only reason that I am as successful as I am is because I failed the way that I did. I don't think I would be as driven as I am or as good of a tutor as I am had I not failed the way that I did. Another of the things that I do on campus is, I work in the learning center, the Academic Center for Excellence, and I'm a math tutor in there but I'm also an academic coach, and what I do is I help freshmen and sophomores when they need help with things on campus. You know, just becoming better students, and I think part of the reason I'm so good at that is because I have failed and succeeded afterward. And so, I think, honestly, I wouldn't be as good at any of the things I do had I not done exactly what I did. But if I didn't want to fail first, I think I would have waited.

I think I would have given myself the time to come to college because I wanted to come to college. But you know, you always hear that story that if you don't go right away, you won't come back. You know, you'll never go, but I'm not one of those people. I'm actually not planning on going to grad school right away, but that's because I'm planning on taking the actuary exams and so everyone's like, "No, you have to go, like, right away," but I'm one of those people that I know I'll go back because I want to, just not right now.

Future Goals

Um, so, I'm actually planning to take the next year off to work and study because I'm planning to take the actuary exams, as I was saying. So yeah ... I think I want to move to Seattle and work as an actuary for an insurance company or something like that. Um, I just love the atmosphere over there. Growing up in California, I'm a big-city girl, so I am definitely interested in that. Seattle is top of my list, you know, but I love Portland and things like that so ...

Um, I just know that taking those exams are really hard. I know that that's not going to be easy whatsoever so I think, just in general, those are going to be my biggest hurdle. But I know I've overcome a lot of hurdles, so as long as can stay focused and things like that, I can ... I can succeed.

Um, I think maybe graduate school is in the future, but it kind of depends on how everything else goes, you know. If I make it to six figures in the future being an actuary and I love it, then I think maybe it won't be necessary unless my company asks me to. But, you know, if I don't like being an actuary or something like that, then absolutely that option is open to me.

Um, we've discussed it a lot. I had to take senior seminar this semester, and we just talked about all the things that we could do with our degrees and the different directions that we could go with it and so that was just one of the things that we discussed and that I decided would be good for me, that I would be interested in.

Advice to Students

Make sure that you're doing it for you, first of all, because if you're doing it for somebody else, it's really hard to do. It's just too hard in general, like overall, colleges are just really difficult to experience. Living at home, being away from home, either way, it's really hard—and then, you know, it's different from high school. Just the whole experience is so different and difficult that if you're not doing it for yourself, you will not succeed. I mean, it's just so difficult. If I had other advice, I would just say to enjoy it, because not enjoying it makes it hard too.

I mean, I actually enjoy college. I'm not going to, like, one of those big schools you see on TV or in a movie or something where there's like fraternities and sororities and parties all the time, but I actually enjoy the college experience. I have met amazing people, and I've had so many opportunities and things like that, so if you actually enjoy the college experience, it's so worth it to be there and to feel that feeling of success and achievement and so …

Advice to Faculty

Um, I would tell them to take the time to know them and to understand what would make them want to be there. You know, if I didn't have that first adviser when I came back actually take the time to make me want to be here, I don't know if I would still be at Tech. He's the reason that I really enjoyed being on this campus, and even though I didn't stay in the department, I still—because I'm in the same building—I still talk to him whenever I see him. I still talk to him about his projects, and had he not taken the time to get to know me and give me that extra little attention, I don't know if I would still be at Tech or in college, for that matter.

Well, he asked me about my grandma, and when he found out my grandma was a software engineer, he always reminded me of why I joined the department. He reminded me of how I could be successful, why I could be successful. He, um, so when I took, uh … there's like a freshman computer science class where you learn to program, you learn Java, um, and basically what you do is you design games, like, basic games … and he used me on, like, the Montana Tech website just because they needed something new, and so he used me to take a picture and to show, you know, the new things they were doing and the program and things like that. He just got me involved in the program, to keep me there, to keep me involved. Because a lot of kids are there, and they want to be there and they are already involved, but I wasn't really until he got me involved.

Intelligence

So I actually had a professor when I was failing out of college, but it was in a writing class and she said a quote to me, and I actually have it tattooed on me because it's one of my favorite quotes, and it says, "When you're green, you're growing; when you're ripe, you rot." And basically, to me, what it means is there's always room to grow, to learn, and to become better. And that's kind of what those words, to me, those little quotes you just gave, you know … there's always room to be better and more intelligent and …

Martin and Patrick

Introductions and Background

Martin: My name is Martin. I'm twenty-four years old. I'm a student at the university. I'm doing my second year in chemistry. I'm the second born in my mother's side of family, but overall, we are seven at home, including both parents. Let me explain that: We have two different mothers. Eugene is my, my youngest uncle, if I may put it like that. The reason being, I'm older than Eugene, with the difference being three months, but then Eugene's mother is my grandmother. And my mother is Eugene's sister. So in my side, my family's side, Patrick's side, in my side, I'm the first born and on Eugene Pritchard's side is the last born of the family. So overall, course we stay together, one family, we are seven in number.

Patrick: Yes! And we grow up together, like we grow up as brothers, and most people like in the community and around us, they actually know us as twin brothers because our age difference is not that much. So we grew up together;

we did everything together; and even at the moment, we are doing the same college.

Starting College/Goals

Patrick: Okay, we started NMMU in 2012. I was twenty-one years by that time.

Martin: Both of us were twenty-one years.

Patrick: We started college at the age of nineteen after we matriculated, and then after that we went to college for two years. One year it was full-time and then the second year, it was part-time. And then after that, we came to the university. And we went to True Harvest College, and that's where we did safety and security for two years.

When we were both going to a college, after ... we wanted to study medicine. We wanted to be American doctors. But because we couldn't get accepted at the university and due to financial reasons, we ended up going to a college. And then after we graduated at the college, we decided what we wanted to pursue ... what we wanted to pursue when we matriculated. We wanted to pursue the dream that we had before, so we came to the university to study a health plan. We just wanted to study something that is related to medicine so that at the end we could get into the medicine field.

Martin: At the moment, it's quite challenging, but we are doing well at the moment. Some challenges are there, but at our academy, we are performing very well.

141

Challenges

Martin: We are from very disadvantaged background of families whereby there was no one who *ever* [emphasis his], ever managed to go to a college or university in the family, so in a way we are the first ones, the first in the family to go to the university. Besides dad, our family, like I said, it's very disadvantaged, whereby our parents, both of them were not working at that moment; they're still not working. They are now dependent on social bonds.

The challenge that we had right then in high school, the fact that we couldn't study more regarding what we wanted before us. It was costly. One reason being our high school, or our secondary school ... just because we're coming from a very disadvantaged background, we were forced to go to the lowest, I mean the very lowest, high schools or secondary schools.

Motivation

Martin: We chose to go to college, reason being financial problem. We had financial difficulties in the family; like I said, no one was working in the family. Our sisters, all the sisters, were pregnant, most of them, so we're like many. And our parents couldn't really focus on our education, reason being they were still having a family or difficulties or having to provide for the family.

But then, what kept us going was the fact that we knew what we wanted to do. And besides the challenges, besides all that we have encountered, besides coming from a very difficult background—we knew that we could do something. We knew that we had the ability to change the situation, and that is what kept us going.

Overcoming Financial Challenges

Martin: Most of the university is having this challenge of financial. The students cannot enroll before the financial difficulty, but what we did as brothers ... in fact, my brother Patrick had to go first before me. He had to study before me. I'm the last one. He's beyond me with one year.

Patrick: I'm doing third year now.

Martin: He's doing third year. I'm doing second year. I had to go to work or find a few jobs for one year. I was doing a one-year job in the retail marketing; whereas, he was studying. And by then, I could help him by buying him food. I could help him by buying him clothes, and I would help him to buy him stationeries; whereas, I was still working and you were at school. And like him, because he was at school, I can say that now that he's the reason why I'm at the university. As I was helping him with finances, he was helping me with finding me a space for a scholarship at school.

More Challenges to Overcome

Patrick: And to add on to that, one of our other challenges that we had to make sure we had the support was the fact that both of our parents, they didn't go to school, and none of our sisters went to school. Our brother dropped out when he was doing engineering at the college due to financial reasons, so that also discouraged us that we cannot get anywhere. But then we kept on motivating each other that no matter what, no matter the circumstances, we can always get to the dream, where we want to get.

And then … the support of the students is one of the basic things that if a student doesn't have that support, they cannot make it in the academic life; so we lacked that kind of support, but we kept on motivating ourselves. That's how we overcame that challenge.

Scholarship

Martin: I had to work very hard so that I could get a scholarship that can pay for my fee. Then I managed to show … that I passed my first year very well, and then I got a scholarship to my second year, and that is the scholarship that is funding me at the moment.

High School Quality

Martin: Most of the classrooms, they are very old classrooms, the ones that have been used by our own father. So the school has a need to be renovated. A number of teachers there at school, the government couldn't provide enough teachers for enough students, especially for math and science. We didn't have a math or science teacher. We only had a math or science teacher for the first quarter of the year; then the other remaining of the year … we couldn't have a math teacher, so we had to study math and science on our own.

A library is like something we had never dreamt of. We never knew the first thing about a library when we were still at the school. It was only after we came to college and to university, that's when we knew that, "Oh! There is something called the library!"

Family Views

Patrick: They're very honored, especially our mother; she's very happy so to say. She always called us each and every day motivating us, telling us to study, telling us to really work hard. She really behind us; that, for us, like we are motivated almost every day because of her, and we can see the reason why she's motivating us. She believes in us. She's really saying that *we* [emphasis his], as brothers, we are the ones to change the situation in the family; we are the ones to bring light into the family; we are the ones to motivate those young ones in the family that are coming after us.

Faculty

Martin: I could say that the lecturers are watching. They are like a family. Though you find some other's way, like you mustn't be afraid to go and talk to them, even if you've got a problem with a certain subject that they are lecturing. But I would say that most of the lecturers, they are like my parents to me. I can go to them whenever I've got a problem or whenever I'm facing a challenge in a subject or in a particular module.

Mentors

Martin: There were mentors at the university. So the university hired mentors to mentor their students who are not working. So they came, and then they motivated me. They established a relationship between me and my lecturer, and then that's how I managed to pass my first year with flying color, if I can put it that way.

The mentors, what they did, they ... each and every subject has what it calls a mentor. The mentors are students, actually, who did very well in that module, but you find out they are in third years and fourth years and they have gone through that course. So the university employs those students and pays them to lecture, to mentor, the first-years and the second-years so that they can also go through what they went through and then also prepare them very well.

Those are the duties of a mentor. And not only that but also to give, to offer emotional support to students, especially the first-years ... Most of the challenges that the students, the first-years and the second-years, encounter, that's where the mentors come in to assist the students.

Support Course: Academic Life Module (ALM)

Martin: ALM. It's like live orientation type of a module where we talk about almost everything that happens throughout our lives ...

Patrick: ... that the students come across ...

Martin: ... and I'd like to commend ... at least one of my lecturers. I really appreciate her, Mrs. C. She's like a mother. In her presence, I can say that she's like—she's not lecturing. It's like she's parenting you. Either way, you feel free whenever you have a problem, whatever problem it might be, big initial problem, psychology type of problem: if you don't perform very well; if you need help; if you're stressed; if you're confused; if there's something happening back at home, she's the right person to ... she always says to us, "Please, come in, talk to me."

Patrick: It gives you a ways to overcome a problem, and if I were to elaborate on that, like it gives you a way that you can break the problem into different pieces and then come up with different ways to solve each and every piece according to its priority.

   Martin: It is divided into categories whereby they teach us about self-concepts: how to look after yourself, how do you take care of yourself. They will teach us communication: how do you communicate whenever you have a problem … how do you communicate; how do you approach … how do you approach a problem in a relationship, conflict management, emotional intelligence, and diversity. It's like: You'll learn more about your life and how to deal with life.

   Patrick: It's also about putting yourself into the shoes of a student: feel what they feel, and be able to interact with the students. And then help them in a certain way that they can also be able to help others and also to help themselves.

Becoming a Student Mentor

Patrick: I want to tell you about this year when I was doing my third year and then last year when I was doing my second year. I am also wearing the T-shirt that, the T-shirt is written, "How to act at NMMU," meaning that we as the mentors, we teach the students how to have academic successes; how to deal with certain issues that they come up with; how to apply for scholarships. So those are the duties of the mentor. I actually had the privilege to be chosen as one of the guys who was to mentor the first year. I did that, and most of the first-years that I come across, like as we move around the university.

147

Advice to Students

Martin: If I were to give advice to students who will be applying to NMMU, I would say that NMMU is one of the best universities in South Africa that I have seen at the moment, looking at the faculties and everything that is there at NMMU. And then I would say to them that they must never give up, like there are so many students applying at the same time. Hundreds might get rejected; hundreds might get accepted, but for those who get rejected, they must never give up to apply to NMMU. Why? Because you never know when will your door open. So I would say that everything that they do in life, they must never ever give up.

Patrick: Believe. Now you believe. Now they felt something within them which is their belief. Now a student has to believe ... not believing in himself ... change. I can bring change. I can be successful. Regardless of where you come from, regardless of your background, regardless of race or culture, you can believe. You can make differences. The only thing that you have to do, even our dean will tell you, that when you get to the university ... when you get to the university, change the mind; change the mind. And that's what they're really trying to do. They change your mind.

Martin: And NMMU teaches you to take responsibility. That is one of the key elements. So you are sure that when you come to visit university, you will have the spirit of open and what it means to you. And then you will have the sense to take responsibility. Look at South Africa as a whole, its median people who are ready to take responsibility; look at the challenges that the country is facing. We need young people who will come up with a new mind for implementing new things. If I were to give an example, at the moment, we are still not sure who will find the cure for HIV. Who knows what might be coming to this university. It might give you other new skills that may enlighten you to think behind the thing; to think out of the box; and then you might end up being one of those who people who come up with the cure for HIV.

Advice to Lecturers

Martin: Lecturers must also put themselves in the shoes of the students. They must be able to teach the students not only academia, but also looking at the life of a student.

Patrick: They should be one, open; two, transparent ... um ... they should be approachable.

Martin: Lecturers should be more open; they should be more understanding.

Patrick: And also accommodating.

Martin: And approachable. If I can't approach you, I cannot talk to you. And if I can't talk to you, I will never understand you. And you'll never hear my story. I'll never be open to you. I'll never tell you what's my problem if you're not approachable. So they must be approachable.

Lecturing is way different; university is different from high school. In a high school, they'll give you a whole lot of notes to write down, and then you'll have to study your notes, but in the university, they just give you the lineup. They just touch here and there, and then you are expected to do the rest. You are expected to do more work, but then we need more than that information. They should be more encouraging as a lecturer.

As a lecturer, I know that the job of the lecturer which is to give us the highlights and the rest is upon us, but then we sometimes have difficulties to do the work because we need, we're lacking that information. So if they can be more accommodating; more informative; more open to their cause and to the modules that they are doing, I think that will help the students more.

Martin: Most of the lecturers, what they will do is that when you make an appointment to meet with them, and that's the obvious thing, they will allow you to come, and then when you go to them, they will listen to your story. Like they will not tell you that, "You know what, we don't have time for this; we are too busy." They will … like, they will have time for you, to listen to your story; to listen to what you have to say; to listen to what it is that you have to bring to the table.

Besides that, I believe that as a lecturer, you are like a parent, so you should have that … how can I put this … the relationship between a student and a lecturer must be like a parent and the child. So, in a way, if you become, like, a lecturer, as you lecture we will not be able to approach you, but we need that somebody we can relate to as a parent, as a father figure, as a mother figure. Because now we come from a different place. We need that someone we can talk to.

Changes Yet to Come

Martin: For me, what I'm concerned about, as we said in the beginning of the interview that our main job is to getting into the medical institute. I see that as the bigger challenge because if we're looking to get our doctor degree, there are only eight major schools. And then we are about a one million population, so you can see that most of the students, they are trying by many means necessary. In South Africa, the shortage of doctors … It's not because the students don't want to study medicine, but it is because the space to accommodate the students for medicine—it's very limited in South Africa.

Patrick: What I want to do right now is to have that stable sponsor for now because I believe that at some point … Of course, I've already encountered so many students who have been like rejected and are now going back home 'cause they are not making finances even though they performed well in academics; it's not planning, so you need to have a stable financial which will help you to achieve your degree. It's hard to get your degree, it's hard to get to the end of your studies, which is four years of … a duration of four years.

Martin: So my plan B is that if I don't get into medical school, I'm going to become a nurse, and then I will be waiting in the hospital until that opportunity arrives.

ABOUT THE AUTHORS

Martha E. Casazza has coauthored two books with Dr. Sharon Silverman: *Learning Assistance and Developmental Education: A Guide for Effective Practice and Learning and Development*. She also coauthored *Access, Opportunity and Success: Keeping the Promise of Higher Education*. She was a Fulbright Senior Scholar to South Africa in 2000 and was an invited scholar to the Kazakhstan-British Technical University in Kazakhstan in 2013. She is a founding Fellow of the Council of Learning Assistance and Development Education Associations.

Sharon L. Silverman is an educational psychologist and a founding partner of TRPP Associates, LLC. She was a Fulbright Scholar in South Africa and a Fulbright Specialist at Suleyman Demeril University in Kazakhstan. She is the recipient of a Rotary International Award for Research in South Africa and the Noel Levitz Retention Award for student success programming.. Along with Dr. Martha Casazza, she co-authored numerous publications, including *Learning and Development: Making Connections to Enhance Teaching.*

REFERENCES

Ambrose, S. A., and M. W. Bridges. 2010. *How Learning Works.* New York: John Wiley and Sons.

Bandura, A. 1986. "The Explanatory and Predictive Scope of Self-Efficacy Theory." *Journal of Clinical and Social Psychology* 4 (3): 359–373.

Barley, Z., H. Apthrop, and B. Goodwin. 2007. "Creating a Culture of High Expectations." *Changing Schools* 55: 5.

Bartimote-Aufflick, K., A. Bridgeman, R. Walker, M. Sharma, and L. Smith. 2015. "The Study, Evaluation, and Improvement of University Student Self-Efficacy." *Studies in Higher Education* 41 (11): 1918–1942.

Bertrando, R. 2014. *Raising the Bar for All Students.* New York: Routledge.

Blackwell, L., K. Trzesniewski, and C. S. Dweck. 2007. "Implicit Theories of Intelligence Predict Achievement across an Adolescent Transition: A Longitudinal Study and Intervention." *Child Development* 78 (1): 246–263.

Bond, C. D. 2012. "An Overview of Best Practices in the Teaching of Listening." *International Journal of Listening* 26 (2): 61–63.

Brooks, J. 2006. "Strengthening Resilience in Children and Youth: Maximizing Opportunities through the Schools." *Children and Schools* 23 (2): 69–76.

Cantrell, S. C., P. Correll, J. Clouse, K. Creech, S. Bridge, and D. Ownes. 2013. "Patterns of Self-Efficacy among College Students in Developmental Reading." *Journal of College Reading and Learning* 44 (1): 8–34.

Di Benedettoa, M. K., and H. Bembenutty. 2013. "Within the Pipeline: Self-Regulated Learning, Self-Efficacy, and Socialization among College Students in Science Courses." *Learning and Individual Differences* 23: 218–224.

Duckworth, A. L., and J. J. Gross. 2014. "Self-Control and Grit: Related but Separable Determinants of Success." *Current Directions in Psychological Science* 23 (5): 319–325.

Duckworth, A. L., C. Peterson, M. D. Matthews, and D. R. Kelly. 2007. "Grit: Perseverance and Passion for Long-Term Goals." *Journal of Personal and Social Psychology* 92 (6): 1087–1101.

Dweck, Carol S. 2006. *Mindset: The New Psychology of Success.* New York: Random House.

Eskreis-Winkler, L., E. Shulman, S. Beal, and A. L. Duckworth. 2014. "The Grit Effect: Predicting Retention in the Military, the Workplace, School, and Marriage." *Frontiers in Personality Science and Individual Differences* 5(36): 1–12.

Esquivel, G., B. Doll, and G. Oades-Sese. 2011. "Introduction to the Special Issue: Resilience in Schools." *Psychology in the Schools* 48 (7): 649–651.

Garmezy, N. 1993. "Children in Poverty: Resilience Despite Risk." *Psychiatry* 56 (1): 127–136.

Gilligan, R. 2004. "Promoting Resilience in Child and Family Social Work: Issues for Social Work Practice, Education, and Policy." *Social Work Education* 23 (1): 93–104.

Goleman, D. 1995. *Emotional Intelligence.* New York: Bantam Books.

————. 2006. *Social Intelligence: The New Science of Human Relations.* New York: Bantam Books.

Goleman, D., and R. Boyatzis. 2017. "Emotional Intelligence has 12 Elements: Which Do You Need to Work On?" https://hbr.org/2017/02/emotional-intelligence-has-12-elements-which-do-you-need-to-work-on (accessed February 6, 2017).

Haimovitz, K., and J. Henderlong. 2011. "Effects of Person versus Process Praise on Student Motivation: Stability and Change in Emerging Adulthood." *Educational Psychology* 31 (5): 595–609.

Henderson, N., and M. M. Milstein. 2003. *Resiliency in Schools: Making It Happen for Students and Educators.* Thousand Oaks, CA: Corwin Press Inc.

Keeling, R., ed. 2006. *Learning Reconsidered 2: Implementing a Campus-Wide Focus on the Student Experience.* Washington, DC: NASPA.

Kotter, J. P. 2012. *Leading Change.* Boston: Harvard Business Review.

Luthar, S.S. & Cicchetti, D. (2000). The construct of resilience: Implications for interventions and social policies. *Developmental and Psychotherapy,* 12, 857-885.

Masten, A. S. 2001. "Ordinary Magic: Resilience Processes in Development." *American Psychologist* 56 (3): 227–238.

O'Dougherty Wright, M., A. S. Masten, and A. J. Narayan. 2013. "Resilience Processes in Development: Four Waves of Research on Positive Adaptation in the Context of Adversity." In *Handbook of Resilience in Children* edited by S. Goldstein and R. B. Brooks, 15–38. New York: Springer.

Pintrich, P. R., and E. V. De Groot. 1990. "Motivational and Self-Regulated Learning Components of Classroom Academic Performance." *Journal of Educational Psychology* 82 (1): 33–40.

Roeser, R., J. Eccles, and A. Sameroff. 2000. "School as a Context of Early Adolescents' Academic and Social-Emotional

Development: A Summary of Research Findings. *The Elementary School Journal* 100: 443–471.

Salovey, P., and J. D. Mayer. 1990. "Emotional Intelligence." *Imagination, Cognition, and Personality* 9: 185–211.

Salovey, P., and D. A. Pizarro. 2003. "The Value of Emotional Intelligence." In *Models of Intelligence: International Perspectives*, edited by R. J. Sternberg, J. Lautrey, and T. I. Lubart, 263–278. Washington, DC: American Psychological Association.

Seccombe, K. 2002. "'Beating the Odds' versus 'Changing the Odds': Poverty, Resilience and Family Policy." *Journal of Marriage and Family* 64 (2): 384–394.

Stoltz, P. G. 2014. *Grit: The New Science of What It Takes to Succeed.* ClimbStrong Press.

Wiggins, G. 2012. "Seven Keys to Effective Feedback." *Educational Leadership* 70 (1): 10–16.

Williams, J. M., and J. Bryan. 2013. "Overcoming Adversity: High-Achieving African American Youth's Perspectives on Educational Resilience." *Journal of Counseling and Development* 91 (3): 291–300.

Williams, N. R., E. W. Lindsey, P. D. Kurtz, and S. Jarvis. 2001. "From Trauma to Resilience: Lessons from Former Runaway and Homeless Youth." *Journal of Youth Studies* 4: 233–53.

Zimmerman, B. J., and D. H. Schunk. 2013. *Self-Regulated Learning and Academic Achievement: Theoretical Perspectives.* New York: Routledge.

INDEX

A

academic integrity, 37
achievement orientation, 38–39
Adam
    about, 9–11
    adaptability, 38
    full interview, 93–103
    grit and, 27–28
    growth mind-set, 31, 52
    parental support, 49
    remedial classes, 4
    self-awareness, 67
    self-efficacy, 43, 45
    social awareness, 40–41
    supportive environment, 53–54
adaptability, 38
Ambrose, S. A., 55
Apthrop, H., 30

B

Bandura, Albert, 42
Barley, Z., 30
barriers to success, ix, 2, 8, 25, 45, 62, 66, 118
Bartimote-Aufflick, K., 46
belief in self, 27, 49, 54, 93, 99–100, 103, 148
Believe in You model, 4–5, 12, 48–50, 61, 64, 69
Bembenutty, H., 46
Bertrando, R., 42
Blackwell, L., 32
Bloom's taxonomy, 87–89
Bond, C. D., 55
Boyatzis, Richard E., 75
Bridges, M. W., 55
Brooks, J., 30
Bryan, J., 30

C

Calvin
    about, 11–13
    emotionally aware, 50
    faculty support, 12–13, 109
    feedback, 54
    full interview, 103–113